The Hollywood Pitching Bible

Third Edition

By

Douglas Eboch & Ken Aguado

SCREENMASTER BOOKS™

Copyright 2013, 2014, 2018 by Douglas Eboch & Ken Aguado.

All rights reserved.

Published by ScreenMaster Books

No part of this publication may be reproduced, stored in a retrieval system, or transmitted in any form or by any means, electronic, mechanical, photocopying, recording, scanning, or otherwise, except as permitted under Section 107 or 108 of the 1976 United States Copyright Act, without either the prior written permission of the authors.

Limit of Liability/Disclaimer of Warranty: While the authors have used their best efforts in preparing this book, they make no representations or warranties with respect to the accuracy or completeness of the contents of this book and specifically disclaim any implied warranties for a particular purpose. No warranty may be created or extended by sales representatives or written sales materials. The advice and strategies contained herein may not be suitable for your situation. The authors shall not be liable for any loss of profit or any other commercial damages, including but not limited to special, incidental, consequential, or other damages.

ISBN: 978-1717242792
ISBN: 1717242790

Cover Art: Julia Chernysheva

For more information or permissions, please contact:

ScreenMaster Books
13535 Ventura Blvd. Suite C #221
Sherman Oaks CA 91423-3891

CONTENTS

PREFACE	vii
INTRODUCTION	ix
WHAT IS PITCHING	1
Why We Pitch	4
The Pitch Experience	5
The Value of an Idea	5
Types of Pitches	7
Pitch vs. Script	9
Learning from Trailers	10
CHOOSING MATERIAL TO PITCH	13
So, You Have an Idea.	14
But, I Gotta be Me	18
Choosing the Right Idea	19
Pick a High-Concept Idea	20
Pick a Marketable Genre	22
Pick an Appropriate Rating	22
Pick an Idea Based on Pre-existing Material	23
Observe the Current Marketplace	25
Pick a Subject That Is Different but Not Too Different	26
Contemporary vs. Period	27
Pick a Subject That Is Life Affirming	28
Pick Characters That Are Inherently Appealing	28
Pick a Trusted Friend	30
Independent Film	31
Picking Material for Television	31
Personal Story: Hell on Wheels by Tony Gayton	35
The X-factor	36
UNDERSTANDING YOUR CONCEPT	39
The Hook	41
Character	43
Personal Story: The Great Debaters by Robert Eisele	46
LET'S CREATE A PITCH	49
Personal Connection	50
Genre, Rating and Tone	61
The Title	61
The Log Line	62
Log Lines: Comparing to Other Movies	78
Introducing the World and Rules	82
Introducing Main Characters	84
Main Characters: Casting Suggestions	86
Plot	88
Plot: The Ending	93
Plot: Using Set Pieces	95
Plot: Using Dialog	96

What about Shorter Pitches?...	98
Gravity: 2-Minute Pitch..	99
Gravity - Version One..	100
Gravity - Version Two..	101
Die Hard: 5-minute pitch...	103
Building Out to a Full-Length Pitch..	107
PITCHING FOR TELEVISION...	109
The Show-Runner...	109
Working in Television...	111
Franchise...	112
Open-Ended or Closed-Ended..	113
Personal Story: The Ghost Whisperer by John Gray............	115
Set Pieces...	119
Pitching Television Movies...	120
Pitching One-Hour Drama and Half-Hour Comedy Series..	120
Animation...	121
What is Reality?..	121
Sample Reality Pitch...	124
PITCHING REWRITES OR ADAPTATIONS.....................................	129
Analyzing the Material and Personal Connection.............	131
Personal Connection..	132
Analysis..	134
Rewrites...	135
Adaptations..	137
PRODUCERS AND DIRECTORS..	139
The Producer Pitch...	140
The Director Pitch...	143
The Director Pitch: Motion Picture..	145
The Director Pitch: Series Television.....................................	146
The Director Pitch: Television Commercials........................	148
Sample Commercial Pitch...	151
PITCHING STYLE AND PRESENTATION..	157
Respect..	157
Confidence..	159
To Memorize or Not Memorize...	161
Don't Look for Approval, Just Tell Your Story.....................	164
Getting Questions and Handling Interruptions..................	165
HOW A MEETING WORKS..	169
General Meetings..	169
Personal Story: Liar Liar by Paul Guay...................................	170
Etiquette..	172
In the Room..	173
One Meeting, One Idea...	175
Pitch Meetings...	176
Wrapping it Up..	177
HOW TO BEHAVE IN A MEETING..	179
Looking Professional..	179
Acting Professional...	179
PROPS AND LEAVE-BEHINDS...	181
Props...	181

Sizzle Reels..	184
Personal Story: Spartacus by Grady Hall.........................	185
Leave-Behinds..	187
CONCLUSION..	191
INDUSTRY SLANG...	193
Genres..	199
PRAISE FOR "THE HOLLYWOOD PITCHING BIBLE"...................	204

Preface

Almost everyone hates to pitch – even those who are good at it. But if you want a long career in the Hollywood creative community, it is a necessary skill to master. It's not a skill that comes naturally to most people and very few film schools teach the subject. As a result, most entertainment professionals begin their careers with no clue how to effectively present their projects and creative ideas. With experience, many of these professionals eventually stumble their way into a workable process, but only after years of anxiety and frustration.

The origins of this book began when we were asked to teach a pitching class at ArtCenter College of Design in Pasadena, California, to address this gap and prepare students for their transition to professional life. After developing and testing a curriculum over several terms, we decided to create this book, both for our class, and for anyone who needs to learn this critical skill. Over the years, we have updated the contents of the book to stay current in an ever-changing business.

For the third edition of The Hollywood Pitching Bible, we are adding additional examples and anecdotes, expanding the scope to cover additional areas of entrainment and emerging media, and updating the information based on recent changes in the industry. But the core ideas remain the same – and the skills and techniques we describe should prove useful throughout any career in the creative side of the entertainment business.

Of course, a book like this doesn't come be without the help of many talented people. We thank Ross LaManna, the Chair of the Graduate and Undergraduate Film Departments at ArtCenter College of Design for planting the seed for this book, and for his ongoing and relentless support for the program we created.

We are also hugely grateful to the following group of supremely accomplished artists who lent us their names, credibility, and wisdom for this expanded third edition of The Hollywood Pitching Bible. They are: Robert Eisele, Tony Gayton, Gary Goldman, John Gray, Paul Guay, Grady Hall, Eric Heisserer, Jeremy Podeswa and Arlene Sanford. These artists contributed illuminating quotes about some of the topics we tackle in the book, and also stories about the pitches they've sold. We think these stories add an invaluable, real-world perspective about the challenges of pitching. Their contributions helped us take the third edition to the next level.

Lastly, we'd like to thank ArtCenter film program graduates Pavan Ojha, Che Thornhill, and Anne Xu for going above and beyond the call of duty with their help and friendship when we were writing this book.

INTRODUCTION

Few people choose to pursue careers as creative professionals because they like sales or are good at selling things. But the ability to explain your ideas and convince people the ideas have merit is crucial to building and sustaining any kind of career in entertainment. Since you are reading this book, we will assume you have already realized this. Maybe you've done some pitches and were disappointed with the result. Maybe you find pitching to be a mysterious and impenetrable process. Maybe both. We're here to tell you that you're not crazy; pitching is really difficult.

You'll notice the title of this book is not "How to Get Rich in Hollywood" or "Pitching for Dollars" or anything like that. We've seen those kinds of books and maybe you have too. Is this because we don't want you to make a good living in Hollywood? Of course not. In fact, we'll guess that some of you are reading this book because you've already read some of those other books and found them lacking. That's where this book will be different. We have over four decades of combined experience, not just selling pitches but also buying pitches. We've been on both sides of the "desk." Perhaps more importantly, we've had many years of experience *teaching* the art of pitching. We think all of this gives us unique insights and qualifications to present the pitching process from the broadest perspective, based on sound aesthetic principles and rooted in the customs of Hollywood. This book will be more than just a list of tricks or a collection of anecdotes.

We will impart some real-world, practical know-how about pitching that we've learned over the decades.

We have a different perspective about the nature and value of learning to pitch from what you might think or have read in other books. We see pitching as an essential skill required for a long-term career in the entertainment business and not a get-rich-quick lottery ticket. We also believe that learning to pitch can be an unexpected pathway to understanding the "DNA" of your own creative ideas. In our approach, we focus on the essential skills of communicating the most compelling aspects of an idea to give you a foundation of knowledge you can build upon.

Think about the variety of projects that get pitched in Hollywood: feature films, television movies, mini-series, one-hour series dramas, half-hour single camera comedies, half-hour situation comedies, television commercials, reality shows, game shows, competition shows, internet programming, documentary programming and more. Now think about all the kinds of material within those varieties: original stories, true stories, adaptations, sequels, remakes, reboots, rewrites and more. Is it possible one book could give you a formula that would apply in all of these scenarios? Unlikely. Instead, we will teach you the fundamental skills of pitching so that you can adapt to whatever situation you might encounter.

Let us summarize our approach to this book and who will get the most from it.

First of all, this is not a book about screenwriting, nor is it a book solely intended for screenwriters. Directors and producers will also benefit from learning to pitch. If you are a writer, we will assume that you already have several scripts or teleplays under your belt and have some experience with the nuts and bolts of creating a fully realized narrative. Maybe you've even sold or optioned one or more of your scripts. If you're a producer or director, you're probably already aware of the need to convince financiers to invest in your projects, actors and crew to choose your project over others, and distributors to distribute the final results.

Further, this is *not* a book about networking, finding an agent, or breaking into the film or television industry – although we will cover aspects of the business that are relevant to all of these areas. This is a book designed to prepare you for when you do get the opportunity to pitch.

We also assume you live in Southern California or New York, or plan to move to one of these places at some point. This is where 90% of all pitching takes place. Lastly, we assume you want to take that next step in your career and that you have some appreciation of the significant differences between a script and a pitch. If not, you will soon learn they are very different things.

For the sake of focus and clarity, we will mostly use the pitching of movies as our recurring examples, though rest assured that we will also discuss pitching television and other media. We will frequently refer to the movies "Gravity" (2013), "Liar Liar" (1997), "The Matrix" (1999) and "Die Hard" (1988) so you will find it helpful to familiarize yourself with these films prior to reading further.

At all steps, we will justify our approach and give a logical framework for the advice we give you. The more you understand the basis for our advice, the more likely you will be able to adapt to the specific situations you will encounter. After you've read this book, the entire process will seem less intimidating and mysterious to you. And maybe, if we are lucky, you will come to understand how learning to pitch can make you a better storyteller. And that's truly our hope.

-Ken & Doug

WHAT IS PITCHING

> "Art is making something out of nothing and selling it."
> -Frank Zappa

Pitching in the entertainment industry is the process by which artistic ideas, points-of-view, and projects are conveyed verbally (and occasionally visually) from one person to another. In many cases, the content of the pitch is a concise summary of a story, told by a screenwriter. Other times, the content of the pitch is the presentation of an approach to a known story. Writers usually pitch with the intention of getting paid to write or rewrite a film or television script, or to adapt something from another medium (such as a book) into one of these things or convince someone to read a completed script. Producers often pitch to sell projects (sometimes with a writer in tow), raise financing, or sell completed films or television projects. Directors typically pitch to get hired on an existing film, television, or commercial project.

Sometimes the person on the receiving end of the pitch is a "buyer." After all, the term pitching is derived from the phrase "sales pitch." Film and television production executives are good examples of buyers.

However, pitching is often (in fact *most* often) done to people who aren't buyers, such as producers, agents, directors, stars and writers. Typically, these people are intermediaries in the process, but the ultimate goal is almost always the same: to get hired or to sell something.

Novice screenwriters frequently think of pitching as the classic scenario where a screenwriter has an original idea for a film or television project, meets with a studio or television executive and summarizes the project they want to write, hoping that executive will agree to buy the pitch and commission the writing of a script. But this is a very narrow view of pitching and in fact it may be many years before a working screenwriter finds him or herself in this classic scenario. Here are some other common pitching scenarios:

- A writer is trying to convince someone to read a screenplay they've already written. This might occur during a casual conversation at a party or industry event, over the phone with a prospective agent, during a general introductory meeting with a producer, or at a pitch-fest type of event.
- A director is pitching him or herself to direct a commercial, film or a television pilot, or an episode of a television series.
- A writer or a producer wants to interest a financier, producer, director or star in an independent film project.
- A writer is attempting to land an assignment to adapt a novel, a comic book, a play or some other source material into a film or television show. Or the writer is trying to get a job rewriting an existing script. In these examples, the writer is pitching their "take" on the underlying material.

- A producer or agent is trying to get *anyone* to read or buy a script, book, series idea, a completed film, or to get a writer hired by pitching something with the writer.
- A writer is proposing a potential episode of a television series to the show-runner, either because the writer is on staff or (much more rarely) to land a freelance assignment.
- A writer is presenting potential "spec script" ideas to their agent or writing partner. In this case, the writer's initial goal is not to get paid, but rather to convince one of these business associates that the writer should invest their time and energy in the idea.
- A director or producer is presenting their idea for a movie to a screenwriter who will pitch or write the proposed script.

As you can see, pitching encompasses a variety of scenarios and purposes. Each can require a different approach with respect to the buyer or listener. By the way, in this book we will use the term "buyer" and "listener" interchangeably when referring to the person on the receiving end of a pitch, but in most cases the listener will *not* be an actual buyer.

The style of pitching we teach in this book is geared towards maximum clarity. In that effort, we teach a fairly regimented format for most pitches. In the real world, the format of your pitch will sometimes differ from what we present in this book, as you adapt your approach to different media, learn the skills, and incorporate your own artistry. This is a *good* thing and it's our hope that, as you learn our building blocks of pitching, you will be able to adapt them to your personal style and to the needs of the individual project.

One more important thought: While learning to pitch has many practical goals, as outlined above, it is also a core principle of this book that learning to pitch can also be a path to better writing and storytelling. Not only will you learn how to present your ideas more clearly, but you can also gain insight about how to *improve* your stories. Pitching does this by requiring you to focus on the analysis of your ideas. Once you understand the DNA of your ideas, it is a shorter step to making those ideas better.

Working in the entertainment industry means you will be immersing yourself in the world of competitive, creative ideas. Learning to pitch, and pitch well, is one of the best things you can do so that you enter the industry with the ammunition you will need to succeed. We want to teach you as many techniques as possible to help you handle all the exciting opportunities that come your way.

Why We Pitch.

> "The only reason I'm in Hollywood is that I don't have the moral courage to refuse the money."
> -Marlon Brando

If you are a writer, you might decide to pitch because, in theory, it takes less time and effort – less of a commitment – to pitch than it would to write a screenplay. And frequently this is true. Certainly, for many well-established writers this is true – but maybe only by a degree. If you're a director or producer, you pitch to get the job or sell one of your projects.

But for a writer, pitching is not as big a time saver as you might think, and when you factor in the time it takes to construct a pitch and then all the time it takes to pitch to the multitude of potential buyers, and then up the food-chain within a company, the timesaving calculus can seem like a frustrating toss-up. But going through this process allows you test out the viability and marketability of your idea as you develop it, rather than doing all the work of writing a screenplay only to find out nobody is interested.

For now, let us all accept that the decision to pitch may not be a decision at all, but rather an unavoidable task that creative people in the entertainment industry will be required to do at one time or another.

The Pitch Experience.

We recognize that for some of our readers the mere thought of pitching seems like a very unnatural pursuit. While a small percentage of people are natural-born raconteurs, the vast majority of them are not. For this latter majority, being the center of attention in a room populated with one or more powerful people in the entertainment industry induces a reaction that can range from mild anxiety to outright terror. We've seen it all, from tiny hand tremors to full-blown panic attacks. Perhaps it's just human nature. If you're a writer, perhaps it has to do with the innate temperament of people who gravitate to the solitary work and lifestyle of that profession. Whatever the reason, you should know that you are in good company and that some of the most successful creative people in the entertainment industry struggle with pitching on a daily basis. Pitching is not easy.

The good news is that we know from years of teaching experience that pitching can be learned. With practice, almost anyone can improve. Once you have a system in place that you know is effective, it will ease your anxiety. And beyond the possible financial incentive of earning a living from doing what you love to do, mastering the art of pitching has the same rewards as any job well done. Nothing succeeds like success. So let's get started.

The Value of an Idea.

Question: What is a great story idea worth?

Answer: Not much.

Are you surprised by that answer? There is a common misperception that a good story idea is an incredibly valuable thing. It's really not.

Professional screenwriters are inundated by people they meet who claim to have a "great idea" for a movie or television show. Usually, what these people want is for the screenwriter to turn their idea into a script and split the anticipated fortune 50/50. Most of the time this great idea is actually *not* that great at all. But even when it is, the truth is most writers have more ideas for movies and television projects than they will ever be able to write in their lifetime. Why should they write someone else's and give that person half the money for the writer's hard work?

Similarly, movie and television companies have no shortage of projects. What they really need are great scripts – and those are rare. Any economist will tell you that price is greatly affected by scarcity. That which is hard to acquire costs a lot. That which is common costs very little.

Likewise, agents and managers aren't really interested in ideas, either. They want clients who can consistently deliver quality work. Breaking a newcomer into the business is labor intensive. Agents seldom make enough money on a first sale or gig for a client to make it worth the effort. They will only do it if they believe the artist is going to generate income for years to come. That's why agents and managers of writers typically want to read two scripts before they sign a new client. And this is why we advise new writers that their second script is more important than their first.

But now we're going to contradict ourselves. It turns out a great idea is actually quite valuable and important – just not on its own.

Movie and television companies shy away from buying a pitch if they feel the writer will not be able to execute the script or if they believe the pitch itself, no matter how well told, is too dependent on successful execution to be worth the risk. Conversely, movie and television companies do not want a well-executed pitch with a bad concept at its core. You need both pieces of the puzzle – a great idea that is well told.

The same does not always hold true for spec screenplays. For example, there have been many spec scripts sold that had strong conceptual ideas but that were under-realized in other aspects. Studios know they always have the option to develop these projects with a new writer, so they can fix any problems in the execution. Indeed, this is the reason why so many scripts get rewritten. But the studio will have the flawed screenplay to give to the new writer. With a pitch, there is nothing tangible to acquire.

Alternately, there are many films that get made where the studio or financier is seduced by the quality of a script's execution, despite reservations about the commercial viability of the core idea. While it's easy to beat up on many of the films that get made in Hollywood and the companies that make them, Hollywood still takes occasional risks on sophisticated and nuanced projects. They just don't develop many of them from pitches.

Producers and directors are also bombarded with movie and scripted television ideas. And often they have ideas of their own they'd like to make. It may be possible to sell these ideas as a pitch if the producer or director is well-established, but even so, the first thing the buyer will do is hire a writer to execute the idea. For less well-established producers and directors, they will have to find a writer themselves to attach to the project. Until there is a screenplay, there is nothing for the producer to produce or director to direct.

Types of Pitches.

Here is a list of frequently used pitch durations and when they are typically used (timing is approximate, of course):

15 to 30 Seconds: The most common length pitch; usually running 2 or 3 sentences. This is often called a log line. (Not to be confused with a "tagline," which is a short slogan used to sell a product. For example, "Long Live the King," for the movie "Black Panther." Taglines are also occasionally used in some longer pitches for "salesmanship" or to "punctuate" an idea.) A log line is most commonly used to get someone interested in reading a script when time is short, such as in an informal social situation. Or it may be used in a meeting when a buyer mentions they are looking for something and you happen to have just such a script. When you have a body of work, it is a good idea to be prepared with a log line for each project. However, a log line is never intended to sell something on its own.

2 to 3 Minutes: Often used in a semi-formal setting where you are trying to interest the listener in an existing project, or a script you have written, such as at a "pitch fest." It isn't a full-blown recitation of the story, but a little taste to make the listener want more. Two-minute pitches can also be used as a back-up pitch (sometimes called a "doorknob" pitch) in a meeting if your longer pitch has crashed and burned. ("Gee, that project is not for us, but what else are you working on?") If the listener finds the doorknob pitch interesting, they may invite you back to hear the full pitch at a later date. Finally, you might use a 2 to 3-minute pitch to convey an idea you are developing to your agent or an executive or producer with whom you already have a relationship. Think of this length pitch as a verbal trailer. Again, it is not intended to sell something on its own. If you've already written a script or have a completed film, there is rarely a need to pitch it for more than two minutes – that is ample time for the listener to decide if they're interested in reading it or viewing it.

5 Minutes: The first pitch on this list to incorporate a significant amount of plotting or artistic perspective (if you are a producer or director). Commonly used in a "general" meeting where the purpose is ostensibly for a buyer to get to know you. At some point, they will want to hear about your next project, which is the cue to give them a 5-minute pitch. (We will discuss general meetings in more detail later.) The advantage of this length pitch is that it gives a real sense of your project without having to initially commit to the work it takes for a full-length pitch. If the listener is interested, they may ask to hear a longer version of the pitch.

10 to 15 Minutes: This is a full-length pitch. Its only intention is to result in someone hiring you to write a script, hire you as the director, or produce your project. Your story idea or "take" will be fully realized, and you are expected to know the answer to any questions the buyer might have thereafter.

Remember, we are not referring to the run time of the *meeting*, but rather just the part where the presenter "has the floor" to pitch. Of course, there are instances where longer pitches are done, but these are uncommon. Fifteen minutes should be adequate time, unless the buyer has specifically asked for a more detailed type of presentation. In most industry situations, going over 15 minutes will only annoy the listener.

In addition to variations in length, there are a few other variations in types of pitches. The approach to pitching an original story is different than pitching to adapt or rewrite. Directors' pitches are different than writers' pitches. Pitching a television series has requirements that are unique to the form. (The term "television" is expanding with the development of streaming and other services. For the purposes of this book, we will use the term "television" to cover any multi-episode narrative or non-narrative programming.) We will cover all of these variations in future chapters.

Pitch vs. Script.

Let's consider what a pitch actually is and how it differs from the final product, such as a screenplay or teleplay. Understanding this difference will make our tips for constructing your pitch feel more logical and less arbitrary.

The most obvious difference is length. If your pitch is 15 minutes long, it can't contain everything that will be in the final 110-page screenplay. If your pitch is only 2 minutes, the problem is magnified. You will have to pick and choose the highlights. You will have to summarize.

Another obvious but important difference is that a pitch is delivered verbally. It is harder for listeners to follow things delivered verbally, especially if the speaker is anxious or rambles. What's vividly clear in your mind may not always be reflected by what you say. The sooner you understand this disconnect, the sooner you will understand the fundamental challenge of pitching. The complexity you might be able to achieve on the page will have to be simplified for the pitch.

On the other hand, because a pitch is delivered verbally and face to face, it can be more interactive. The listener can ask questions or ask you to elaborate if they have concerns or don't understand something or are taken with a particular aspect of your idea. This can be a huge advantage for the pitcher – if they are prepared.

It might be more helpful to say that a well-executed pitch is *analogous* to the final product. One is not merely a shorter version of the other. The act of pitching and the act of writing are derived from different skill-sets. And this is why so many writers have trouble with pitching, and why the best writers are rarely the best pitchers.

Learning from Trailers.

Try this exercise. Pick a recent movie you know well that is also similar to the kind of film you want to pitch. Go online and find the trailer for the movie, then study how the distributor tackles their pitch. After all, a trailer is really nothing more than the "audio-video" version of a *2-minute* pitch designed to get you to want to see a film.

The people who make trailers do it for a living and some are quite good. Study the things the trailer emphasizes: how it presents the concept of the film, how much time it spends developing the characters, how it introduces the setting, the spectacle, the comedy or drama, the "attitude," how it summarizes the plot, and how the trailer "sells" what's cool or compelling about the film. Does the trailer accurately reflect what you know the film to be? Does it represent what you loved about the film?

We are not saying you will be pitching the trailer for your final product. There are significant differences between a pitch and a trailer. For example, most pitches over 5 minutes will include a fairly complete outline of the story: beginning, middle and end. Whereas only a truly misguided trailer would give away the ending to the film it's selling. In this regard, a trailer has similar ambitions to a 2-minute verbal pitch. Trailers, as with 2-minute pitches, tend to emphasize the "sizzle" rather than the "steak." In other words, they will emphasize the excitement of anticipation, as opposed to the labor of cutting and chewing. Trailers are a kind of tease and, in fact, shorter trailers are often called "teasers."

The compelling quality of trailers has led to a Hollywood term called "trailer moments." A trailer moment is an intentionally exaggerated or rousing bit in a pitch or script intended to help the buyer visualize a similarly cool or compelling bit in the trailer when it comes time to sell the film.

On a related note, we've all seen great moments in trailers that end up missing from the finished film. This may be because the trailer was made while the film was still in a longer, unedited form. In a way, this is perfect metaphor for the difference between a pitch and its final product. In fact, a good pitch will frequently include details that may never end up in the final product. Ironically, this is done for clarity and not deception. We will soon see why this is so.

CHOOSING MATERIAL TO PITCH

> "Those are my principles, and if you don't like them... well, I have others."
> —Groucho Marx

As we've said, pitching an original idea may not be the most common type of pitch, but it's the type most people think of when they think of pitching. Also, it's the type of pitching where the writer exerts the most control because the story usually originates in the writer's head. We will cover other pitching scenarios and there will be plenty of overlap, but first we will focus on the process of choosing the subject of your original pitch.

If you're a writer and planning to develop an original pitch, choosing the right subject matter is certainly one of the most important decisions you will make. This is also true if you're planning to write an original screenplay or teleplay – even more so given the additional time and effort these things may take to execute. And while this book focuses on pitching, some of the same considerations apply to the creation of both an original pitch and an original screenplay, especially when you consider that you may end up having to pitch your completed screenplay at some point. So choose carefully.

Not every viable idea can be pitched easily in 15 seconds. Some ideas require more context and detail to prove their appeal. And some ideas will be almost impossible to sell as a pitch, being deemed as "execution dependent" – that is, only viable if a script has already been fully realized. Understanding this will help you determine which ideas might be saleable as a pitch and which probably need to be turned into a spec screenplay. But since we have just said that you will still need to pitch your spec screenplays, we will also discuss how to identify the most compelling, "pitchable" elements of your story throughout this section.

Finally, it will be impossible to sell an original idea as a pitch until you have demonstrated a previous ability to execute similar ideas. For example, as a writer, you must have a sample screenplay that shows your writing ability. Directors and producers can sometimes sell original ideas with the assumption that a writer will then be hired to create the screenplay, but this is only possible once the director or producer has established their own skills in their respective fields.

So, You Have an Idea.

Not every idea that pops into your head at two in the morning will be a flash of brilliance. There is a famous anecdote about the writer who believes that great movie ideas come to him in the middle of the night, in his dreams. But when he wakes up he can never recall the details of the brilliant idea – the haze of sleep having wiped the memory clean. So the writer decides he will leave a pad of paper and a pen on the nightstand and write down the idea when it comes to him. In the morning, there will be a record of the brilliant idea.

One night, the writer awakens at two in the morning with a brilliant story idea. He quickly writes it down and goes back to sleep.

The next morning the writer awakens, as usual. He eats breakfast and when he's brushing his teeth he remembers he had a dream. The writer races to the nightstand, and there on the pad of paper is written the words, "Boy meets Girl."

The point of the story is that not every idea you have will be a pearl and even if it is a pearl, not every pearl is a pitch. Often ideas do not sell as a pitch not because the pitch is poorly done, but rather because the idea being pitched is flawed in some way.

In fact, the irony of learning to pitch is that the more you improve, the more apparent the flaws will become in the story you are pitching. If you think about it, this makes perfect sense. The less the listener has to struggle to understand your presentation, the more they will be able to focus on the content of what you are saying. The flip side of this irony is that it also contains within it an opportunity to become a better storyteller and even a better writer. The process required to formulate a pitch provides you with an opportunity to analyze and improve the elements of your story.

To some readers this might seem counter-intuitive because many regard pitching as merely a way to summarize the story they've already worked out in their heads or a script they've already written. This is exactly backwards, and it can result in stories that are under-realized in some fundamental way. You would be amazed how often we hear pitches and read scripts where it is clear to us the storyteller does not understand their own story and what is best about it. Learning to pitch can be an invaluable way to analyze the DNA of an idea as a path to understanding it, reverse-engineering it, and perfecting it. As we've mentioned, this is a core principle of this book.

There is a misconception among beginners that a pitch is merely a plot summary of what the final product will be. And while this may be true on a superficial level, successful pitching requires a deeper understanding of the differences between your pitch and your intended final product.

A fully executed screenplay contains every line of dialog and a detailed description of every location and action. More importantly, it embodies the sum total of the narrative momentum that is usually only possible in a fully realized screenplay. So, for example, in the movie "The Blind Side," the pleasure we get from seeing Michael Oher committing to play football for Ole Miss at the end is a direct result of the two hours we just spent watching him strive to reach this moment.

Imagine the difficulty of conveying the emotional experience of Michael's challenges in 30 seconds and you will come to understand the problem. Even in 15 minutes, it just might not be possible to convey all the ups and downs of the character's struggle in a way that is meaningful. Does this mean a story like "The Blind Side" is tough to pitch? Maybe, and in fact "The Blind Side" was based on a book by renowned author Michael Lewis. But regardless of the story, the essential nature of the challenge is clear: you need to find a concise way to shorthand the experience of the final product and why it will have special merit. After all, you're trying to convince someone to pay you a significant amount of money for you to take what's in your head and execute a fully realized screenplay. That's a big leap of faith for a buyer. If you can't get them to "see" the film, there's almost no chance they will buy your pitch.

Let's over-simplify this point for the sake of clarity. If you're pitching a film that will be a comedy, is your pitch funny? If you're pitching a drama, will the pitch make the listener cry? If it's an action film, will your pitch be exciting? If it's a horror film, will the pitch be terrifying? It seems self-evident that this should be true, but you might be amazed how rarely it happens in the real world.

Let's expand the point from there. What's the central idea of your story? Can it be summarized in 30 seconds? Can it be summarized in 15 minutes? Let's use the example of "The Blind Side" again. Does your pitch rely on the nuances of understanding the subculture of high school football? Or, do you really want to tell the story of a troubled young man and a compassionate woman whose generosity is put to an extreme test? Maybe your story is more about Michael's character transformation and less about his athletic ability.

If you understand this example, you will start to realize why picking a pitch-appropriate subject matter is so critical and why a simple plot summary is never adequate for a successful pitch.

Before we get to some tips for picking the right subject matter, it's important to point out that the choice of what to pitch will often *not* be a choice at all. For example, when pitching a rewrite or an adaptation, the writer typically plays no role in choosing the subject matter. Similarly, if a director is pitching to get hired, their pitch will almost always be based on something that already exists and possibly moving towards production. As we said in the introduction, the intention of this book is for the reader to understand pitching from the broadest perspective, and in this case, it means there may not always be a whole lot of artistic freedom in what you end up deciding to pitch. Later in this book we will deal with the special challenges of pitching assigned material, but astute readers will see that some of the following commercial and aesthetic considerations for choosing the right subject matter can be helpful in other pitching situations – even ones where you *didn't* choose the subject matter!

But, I Gotta Be Me.

Sooner or later most working writers, directors and producers will have to grapple with this fact of life: Unless you are independently wealthy, what you decide to pitch will be driven by forces in the marketplace and, on a more basic level, the human need for food and shelter. Put another way, getting paid as a filmmaker can be less about originality or inspiration and more about hard work. Put yet another way, success is 1% inspiration and 99% perspiration. At least that was how Thomas Edison saw it, and he was a pretty successful guy. We have no idea what kind of filmmaker Edison would have been and we can debate the relative percentages in his equation, but the point is this: get used to the idea that what you will pitch and write may not always be determined solely by your personal artistic passions.

Sure, there are plenty of situations where a writer has some offbeat or esoteric original story burning inside him or her, a story they just *have* to tell, damn the skeptics! And while we would never diminish the value of personal artistic expression, and have seen it bear fruit on occasion, most working writers will tell you this is not the kind of writing that routinely pays the bills over the course of a career. You go where the jobs are. Spend months or years of your life developing your original passion project only to hear comments like, "I don't understand it" or, "It doesn't seem commercial" or, "That's not the sort of film we make" and you will probably adjust your perspective very quickly.

Once again, we are not dismissing the value of passion in a writer's career. Often, it's the passion for a story that can be the way a writer will establish their personal "voice" – a unique perspective or sensibility. As screenwriter Robert Eisele ("The Great Debaters") puts it, "No indelible line separates high-concept ideas from stories that depend on the writer's talent and execution. When I'm pitching ideas that are more execution dependent, I try to compensate by infusing the pitch with more depth and passion. And never underestimate the power of genuine enthusiasm." With a spec script, this personal voice can be especially valuable. Even if the spec doesn't sell, it may be the script that helps a writer get noticed in a crowded field.

When a writer, director, or producer decides to pitch a project, he or she needs to choose what they pitch with an eye toward the marketplace. And even then, they must be flexible. While it is insulting to say that good story ideas are "a dime a dozen," it's also true that story ideas are the business of Hollywood, and Hollywood's in the "volume business." There will be many pitching situations where your initial idea, the one that you've been burning to tell, just isn't right for a particular buyer, and it will not necessarily have anything to do with the artistic quality or even the commercial viability of the idea. Just remember, don't get hung up on having any one idea to pitch. If you find that one story isn't working for you, well, you'll have others.

Choosing the Right Idea.

Now we are ready to get into the specifics of how you select appropriate material and start to build a pitch. When you work in Hollywood, the things you pitch do not exist in a vacuum. As with any business there are practical considerations you must understand so you have the greatest chance at success. You might know how to build a house, but no professional builder will start building unless they are sure the ground beneath them is solid.

We will initially focus on choosing an idea for an original motion picture story, then we will discuss choosing ideas for television. A little later in the book we will cover the additional considerations for director pitches and other pitching scenarios. As you will see, there is a good amount of overlap.

Here are a few tried and true guidelines to help you select the best subject matter.

Pick a High-Concept Idea.

In the motion picture business, it is both conventional wisdom and 100% true that it is much easier to pitch and sell story ideas that are "high-concept." High-concept is a commonly-used, but sometimes misunderstood, phrase in Hollywood. It refers to a story idea that can be both summarized *and* made to sound intriguing in one or two sentences. That last part is very important. The notion of high-concept speaks to a certain "commercial" quality of an idea – an idea that can be briefly described and will be instantly recognized for its popular appeal. Of course, many ideas can be summarized in one or two sentences, but that doesn't make them high-concept. It's possible to describe the wonderful, character-driven film "Lady Bird" in a couple of sentences, but there's no version that will approach high-concept. Or, for example, "A man robs a bank" is a one sentence description but not very high-concept. On the other hand, "A quadriplegic hostage is actually the mastermind behind an elaborate bank heist and revenge plot" comes closer to being high-concept.

Note how the high-concept version takes the fundamental component of the first version ("man robs bank") and augments it with several specific bits of intrigue and detail. It's no longer just a man, but now he's a quadriplegic. And he starts as a hostage but is really the mastermind! And it's no longer just a robbery but rather a *heist* for the purpose of *revenge*! All this crammed into one little sentence. These added bits of intrigue – the things that complicate or amplify the stakes – are referred to as the "hook" of the concept. This last version of the concept is pretty close to what we might use for a 15-second "elevator pitch." (The term elevator pitch refers to the log line you pitch Steven Spielberg if you happen to share a 15 second elevator ride with him. Though should you find yourself in that situation, we wouldn't recommend pitching Mr. Spielberg. Doing so is more likely to get you labeled a stalker than a writer.) We will revisit the importance of the hook a little later in this book. You will see it is a key aspect of storytelling in Hollywood.

Keep our above sample heist concept in mind. We will continue to refer back to it and build upon it as we move forward in this book. One other point about this sample concept – you might notice that it contains some plot twists that would likely not be revealed so readily in a longer version of the pitch (that the quadriplegic hostage is actually the mastermind). This fact is a perfect illustration of another core principle of this book – different length pitches have very different ambitions.

The notion of high-concept is sometimes misleadingly conflated with the terms "one-liner" and "log line." (In fact, "log line" and "one-liner" are often used interchangeably in Hollywood, but there are some differences.) As previously explained, high-concept refers to an idea that is both succinctly expressed and very intriguing, with broad appeal to a large segment of the audience. This quality is ideally embodied in a single sentence (which is how the misleading term "*one*-liner" originated) but it doesn't have to be just one sentence. Trying to boil a story down to just one sentence is often a pyrrhic victory that comes at the price of clarity.

That said, if someone in Hollywood asks you for your one-liner or log line, they are really asking for the shortest expression of your idea that embodies both what it's *about* and what's *cool* about it. Explicit to the question is that they want it very *brief*. Implicit to the question is that commercial ideas *can* be expressed briefly. If your answer to the question takes several rambling minutes, you just blew it. On the flip side, if your answer is short, but without embodying the commercial considerations, you also blew it. So, for example, if you answered, "It's about World War II," or to use our sample story, "A guy robs a bank," that's not what they're asking. Both of these ideas are too vague and general to be of value.

A log line can be *any* short description of a story or idea – it need *not* be high-concept. A log line might also appear in a synopsis of a screenplay, in TV Guide listings, or the catalog of a film festival, and while some of them may be high-concept, many are not.

The notion of high-concept is typically *less* important in scripted television pitches, where things like series "franchise" and compelling characters are more highly valued. (In Hollywood, the term "franchise" means different things, depending on whether you are talking about television or film. We'll explain the various uses of this term later in this book, but the term is also defined in the glossary at the end of this book.)

Pick a Marketable Genre.

This is another fundamental decision to make when selecting a story to pitch. Is it a comedy? A drama? A horror movie? A psychological thriller? A suspense film? Is it some combination of these things? Identifying your film's genre is crucial because this will determine one of the most basic ways in which your final product will be categorized in the marketplace.

If you're a beginner, be aware that the Hollywood creative community has its own terminology when it comes to describing genre and sub-genre. You'll find a partial list of these at the end of this book.

One note of caution: we live in an era of multi-genre "mash-ups," and there's nothing wrong with this. But if you start describing your project as a blend of too many genres, it can get a little silly. Try explaining to your agent that you want to pitch a "science fiction-action-comedy-drama" and watch your agent's eyes glaze over. Too many genres mixed together will become no genre. Pick, at most, the two predominant genres and let your pitch say the rest. If you're new to showbiz, be aware that Hollywood has its own industry-specific terminology for the various genres. At the end of this book, we provide a list of examples. With this in mind, let's call our heist example a "suspense-thriller."

Pick an Appropriate Rating.

If you're pitching a movie idea, what MPAA rating do you think the final film will deserve? Is it an R-rated comedy? Is it a PG-13 action film? Are you planning a G-rated family film? All of these choices can have a positive or negative impact on the odds of your selling your pitch. A few obvious examples: Try selling a G-rated film to anyone except Disney – and even they don't make many. Or, try selling your explicit NC-17 film to, well, *anyone*.

In the U.S., television has its own unique rating system, but no one uses that ratings system when pitching. However, there are some equivalent terms. For example, you might refer to your idea as a "10 pm series" (for a gritty adult series), or a "prime-time series" (suitable for the entire family), or a "premium cable series" (for sex, language and violence), and so on. Of course, if you are pitching to a network or cable company, they know exactly what kinds of programming they buy, so specifying this is unnecessary. We'll cover this topic in more detail in our chapter about television.

If you're pitching a film, you should be able to identify at least five or six *successful* films in your genre and with a similar rating released within the last five years. If not, it probably means the buyers will not be in the market for that genre. Let's say our heist film is going to be an R-Rated film. This is Hollywood code for saying that the violence will be fairly graphic, there will be darker themes, and likely profanity. A few examples of recent, successful, suspense-thrillers that are rated R are "Baby Driver," "Hell or High Water," "The Girl on the Train," "Sicario," "Gone Girl," "Prisoners," and "John Wick." So far, so good.

Pick an Idea Based on Pre-Existing Material.

Not every story has to be based on your original ideas. Basing your pitch on previously existing source material, such as a novel, newspaper article, a true story, or comic book, can be a great way to go. There are several advantages. Source material can give you a head start with a good story, and many writers choose this path if they are not adept at coming up with their own good, original ideas. Another advantage: when you walk into the pitch meeting, you are coming in with more than just what's between your ears. This can make your project seem more substantial. It is also conceivable that your source material will have a pre-existing, built-in fan base. This is why so many film and television projects get made that are based on best-selling books, comics, toys, and other forms of well-known intellectual property. Of course, it's unlikely a beginning writer will be able to get their hands on a bestselling *anything* because of the prohibitive cost of doing so.

True stories can also be a good source of material for Hollywood. In theory, no one owns a true story. In reality, you can get into trouble with issues of so-called "life rights" and other legal aspects. Be careful and consult an entertainment lawyer.

You might be able to find a viable project based on a well-known story or character that is in the public domain. Works in the public domain are free from the usual restrictions of copyright law. American copyright law emanates from the US Constitution and protects the rights of authors to control and profit from their works, but not forever. When those rights expire, anyone may freely use the work created by the author, including its story and characters.

Note that we said "well-known story or character." There are countless stories and characters in the public domain, but if you pick one that is obscure, it will not give you any advantage in marketability. Unfortunately, determining what is in the public domain is not always easy. Yes, The Holy Bible is a pretty safe choice, as are the works of Shakespeare. But determining what qualifies as public domain can be tricky; different countries have different laws for determining what is in the public domain. Again, be careful and consult an entertainment lawyer.

And this brings us to the challenges of using pre-existing source materials. It is not recommended that you ever base your pitch on any source material where the right to use that source material is in question. The acquisition of rights is beyond the scope of this book but if this is something you really want to pursue, once again, we recommend that you consult with an entertainment attorney. Our heist story is an original idea so we own all rights. Nice and simple.

Observe the Current Marketplace.

Another barometer of your idea's marketability is to compare your story to the kinds of things that are selling to buyers in the film and television marketplace. This is closely related to choosing a marketable genre. We are amazed at how rarely writers, producers, and directors consider this factor when evaluating the chances for their original ideas. Trends do come and go in the kinds of things that buyers want to develop and it's often based on what is currently working in the marketplace. It's also important to point out that every writer should be aware of films and television shows that are in production or scheduled for release. There are few things more embarrassing (and demoralizing) than pitching your project only to have the buyer say, "Great idea, but we have that same film coming out later this year." The best way to know what's getting bought and made is to read the Hollywood industry trade publications religiously. The three best known are *Variety*, *The Hollywood Reporter*, and *Deadline Hollywood*. There are also numerous websites and blogs that track industry-oriented information, news and script sales. Some of the top free industry web sites include The Wrap (thewrap.com) and Vulture (vulture.com). There are also several notable pay-sites, including the Internet Movie Database Pro (pro.imdb.com), Done Deal Pro (donedealpro.com), and The Studio System (getstudiosystem.com).

The analysis of the marketplace as the basis of predicting the marketability of your pitch is a very complex challenge. If what *is* working were always a clear indicator of what *will* work, nobody would ever make a flop. Sometimes it's the exception that works best. And it may take a year or a decade before a pitch becomes the final product, and who knows what the audience will want at that time. Still, an analysis of what's working in the marketplace is highly recommended if only because your pitch is likely to be evaluated in this way when you meet with a buyer. While our sample heist film is in a popular genre, we looked around and could find no one else developing or producing a similar film. But one may come along tomorrow, so we will keep checking.

Pick a Subject that is Different but not too Different.

Closely related to evaluating the current marketplace is the judgment you will have to make about whether your project is similar or unique when it is compared to what's come before. So, for example, if the hit film "Taken" and its successful sequel are the model for your pitch, does the comparison still work if your pitch involves space aliens doing the "taking"? Or does this one twist make your pitch too far removed to make a reasonable comparison?

It is an old bit of wisdom that success comes from taking the familiar and repackaging it in some fresh way. For example, "28 Days Later" took the conventional, lumbering zombie film but made the zombies fast – and made the real villains other people. "Shaun of the Dead" used the same genre but made the heroes two slackers and added social satire. More recently, the hit series "The Walking Dead" took the well-worn genre and made it fresh again by returning the subject matter to the original human drama roots that made the 1968 film "Night of the Living Dead" so compelling.

Everything old is new again. The buyers want "familiar but different." Keep in mind, especially if you are a newer writer, you must offer them something fresh. When a movie is a surprise hit, it's common that everyone in Hollywood will suddenly be looking for something similar. After "Girls Trip" became a hit, many studio execs were looking for female-driven, raunchy comedies – and many writers were pitching them. In order for the buyer to pick yours, you have to offer some intriguing variation, not simply a knockoff. Looking at our sample heist film, we think the twist of having a quadriplegic as the mastermind – a very unlikely "antihero" – is a unique spin on a venerable genre.

Contemporary vs. Period.

If you polled executives at any of the networks or studios and asked what they are looking for, many would say, "We are open to anything, but we really don't want period."

The definition of "period piece" is a little tricky but we would characterize it as any project where the vast majority of the setting is not contemporary or doesn't *look* contemporary. There are many reasons for Hollywood's aversion to films and television shows with period settings. For example, some executives believe that the demographically important younger members of the audience will not relate to time periods that pre-date their lives. Also, a non-contemporary setting can dramatically increase the budget. If you have a street scene set in 1990, for example, it's not just a matter of finding cars from that era but also removing every car made since then, not to mention redressing cell phone stores, removing Viagra advertisements, and so on.

To be sure, period pieces like "Dunkirk," "It," "Beauty and the Beast," "Hidden Figures," and the "Pirates of the Caribbean" movies can be very popular with audiences. And there are many recent examples of successful television series with period settings, including "The Marvelous Mrs. Maisel," "Mindhunter," "Stranger Things," "Masters of Sex," "Vikings," "The Americans," and even sitcoms like "The Goldbergs" and "Fresh Off the Boat." But if you are attempting to sell a period piece, you will need to justify the reason it must be set in the past – with a commensurately higher budget. "Wonder Woman" was set during World War I, and it used the backdrop of the war as a core element of the story. On the other hand, there would be no good reason to set movies like "Baby Driver" or "The Big Sick" any time but the present. Of course, there are some stories that are set outside familiar human timelines, such as science fiction and fantasy stories. "Game of Thrones" and "Star Wars" come to mind, but any pitch based on stories like these will need to justify the additional potential production costs. Our sample heist film is contemporary so this is not an issue.

Pick a Subject that is Life-Affirming.

This is the biggest cliché on the list but probably the most consistently true. Almost without exception, Hollywood prefers to supply its audience stories that affirm the value of the human condition. In practical terms, this typically means happy endings, characters that triumph over adversity, characters that learn from their mistakes, and evil that does not go unpunished. If the main character dies, which almost never happens, they usually do so for some greater good, or to pay penance for doing something bad. If this sort of thing doesn't appeal to you, please consider another profession or, at the very least, don't plan to sell your story from a pitch.

So let's consider this in reference to our sample heist idea. While we think there is some moral ambiguity in our story (after all, our quadriplegic, while sympathetically afflicted, is also a bank robber), the guilty will not go unpunished. We will make sure that's clear.

Pick Characters that Are Inherently Appealing.

This is closely related to the previous advice but it's worth reemphasizing because of how often beginners don't seem to understand or care about it. This may be a byproduct of an exploitation subgenre produced by Hollywood – mostly in the horror genre – where characters are not so much people as they are props to be killed off in imaginative and gory ways. In any case, we've yet to hear any writer justify their unappealing characters with this sort of example.

To be clear, we are not suggesting you only develop pitches that must be cast with irrepressible nice-guy actors like Tom Hanks. There is nothing wrong with a story that has characters with flaws. Many hit movies and television shows have characters that are not exactly likeable or heroic, but in all cases, there should be a reason we care about them and root for them. If your story requires the listener to endure an unpleasant, seemingly unredeemable protagonist for most or all of the pitch, you have a steep hill to climb. Try to create a main character that the listener will care about. Give the listener a reason to sympathize with your main character, and make sure you include it in any pitch. There are many ways to accomplish this and most of the better books about screenwriting will explain how it's done.

Let's look at our sample pitch with this in mind. Based on our one-liner, it seems that our lead (the quadriplegic) may not be such a good candidate for the leading man. Even if he was wronged in the past, that may not justify putting the lives of hostages at risk. So let's reconfigure our story a bit. How about this: "A loan officer befriends a quadriplegic customer only to discover his new friend is the mastermind behind an elaborate heist and revenge plot." In this revised version we now have a new hero, the loan officer, who just happens to be in the wrong place at the wrong time. Very sympathetic.

Is this change better or worse? Did we violate some core artistic principle by making this change? We don't think so: the conceptual hook (quadriplegic as criminal mastermind) still remains. And the upside is that there will be no ambiguity about the appealing nature of our hero. To be clear, it may have been possible to have our quadriplegic bank robber as the hero. We can all cite numerous films and television shows that have "anti-hero" main characters. "Ocean's 11" or "Breaking Bad" come to mind. If we had gone this route, we would have had to work harder to get the listener rooting for our hero. We didn't want to make our job harder, so we altered our idea. This change is a good example of the flexibility we recommend when crafting your pitch. It is also a great example of the value of perfecting your story idea *in advance* via the pitching process as a way to help you understand the best version of your story and the DNA of your idea. We encourage you to keep an open mind as you go through this process, especially at this very early stage of development. It's hard enough to craft a viable story and pitch. Don't paint yourself into a corner.

Pick a Trusted Friend.

This final tip is so important that it almost deserves its own book. Anyone who intends to develop a pitch, indeed anyone who plans to pursue a career as a writer, director or producer, must develop a network of trusted friends. These trusted friends will be the people you rely upon from time to time to give you unbiased feedback about your ideas and stories. Often, these trusted friends will end up being other filmmakers who will in turn ask you to provide the same service for their ideas. The value of trusted friends is much more than just having someone to act as a test audience while you pitch out loud for the first time. Unbiased feedback from a trusted friend can make a dramatic difference in your ability to distinguish a good idea from a bad idea, what's working and what's not. The reason this is true, and so important, evolves from the solitary nature of creating ideas. Storytellers spend long days, weeks, or even months alone in a room, developing their ideas. Under these circumstances, it's not unusual to lose some objectivity. The nature of the problem can be summed up in three words: "everyone loses perspective." Recall that we said not every idea is a pearl and not every pearl is a pitch. Having a trusted friend can be the first line of defense in your ability to know the difference.

Finding the right trusted friend is not always easy. There are three basic requirements:

1) A trusted friend is just that: someone who is "trusted," not only for their confidentiality, but who will also take the time to care and listen.

2) Someone who is knowledgeable enough to give you articulate feedback. This is why the friend is so frequently another writer, producer, or director. Regardless, it should be someone who understands what constitutes a viable story idea and has some insight into the creative process.

3) Someone who will give you honest feedback. Hollywood is a place that can kill you with kindness. After all, most people, and even most friends, will be disinclined to give you honest criticism if they know you just spent a month of your life working on your pitch. It's much easier for friends to tell you what they think you want to hear. To solve this problem, you will need to cultivate working relationships with your trusted friends that encourage and accept their notes and criticisms. This means not getting mad at your trusted friend for their (sometimes brutal) honesty. Conversely, you should try to learn to tell the difference between polite compliments and genuine enthusiasm. There is a huge chasm between, "Sure, that sounds good" and, "Wow, that's great!"

Good feedback from a trusted friend can be the difference between success and failure.

Independent Film.

The above tips are primarily a guideline for picking material to pitch feature films to mainstream Hollywood studios, but the independent and "art film" market operates by surprisingly similar principles. There are some subject matters that are popular at Sundance and some that aren't. Period films are often tougher to get made in the independent world because of the additional expense. High-concept can be less important for an art film, but the bar for a fresh take is comparatively higher. Be aware that few pitches are sold in the independent film world – they almost always start with a spec script. However, if you go the independent route you will still find yourself pitching your story to potential talent and financiers. You will quickly find they are no more interested in making a flop than the studios.

Picking Material for Television.

All of the guidelines we've discussed for choosing subject matter in a motion picture pitch also apply to television projects in general, but there are a few additional considerations, including things like format, franchise and branding.

What Format: When choosing a subject matter in television, the most obvious additional consideration lies in the variety of formats that are programmed. The common television formats for scripted programming include half-hour comedy series, one-hour drama series, two-hour television movies, and limited-series (sometimes known as mini-series).

There are also reality and non-fiction series programmed on television. Reality programming (sometimes referred to as "unscripted" television) is a vast and diverse subset of non-fiction television that includes home renovation shows, cooking shows, celebrity shows, competition shows, and many more sub-categories. Some reality programs are in a half-hour format, but most run for one-hour, including ad time.

Of all these television formats, only the two-hour television movie pitch bears a close resemblance to a film pitch. The other formats will require you to pick and tailor your subject matter in a way that is very specific and different from films. Let's examine why.

Most Hollywood films run about two hours. Some films run longer – mostly those with epic subject matters or self-indulgent directors at the helm, or both. A handful run shorter, mostly family films intended for children or certain "genre films" (horror films, comedies, etc.) usually intended for a teenage audience. Interestingly, the topic of running time almost never comes up in a feature film pitch meeting, where it is universally assumed that the running time of the project being pitched will be about two hours, more or less. Nevertheless, a movie writer has a fair amount of liberty when it comes to the scope of the narrative.

On the other hand, ad-supported television is much more restrictive, and the running times of the various formats will have a fundamental impact on the kind of story you are able to pitch. Every network executive and every network television writer, director, or producer will know exactly how long their final product will run, often down to the second. There are some minor exceptions to this rule in cable television – channels like Showtime, FX, AMC and HBO. The running times on these channels sometimes vary by two to five minutes. Then there are series delivered over the Internet from companies like Netflix, Hulu, Amazon, and iTunes. For most of these "content providers" running time is not an issue, although their shows still tend to keep their episodes in either the 30-minute or 60-minute ballpark.

Regardless, if you are planning to pitch in television, then choosing the format will probably be the first decision you make.

Ongoing Story Lines: The second additional consideration when picking a subject matter for television is that most television series contain ongoing stories and characters. This is true of both scripted programming *and* some reality programming, although of course reality characters are "real" people. In practice, this means it's very likely the story you pitch for television will not have a clearly defined or resolved end point. Imagine our sample heist film as an on-going series and the problem will become obvious. Is it really plausible we could create a series that returns to the same hostage scenario on a weekly basis for years? (Although the 2013 series "Hostages" tried something similar to this. It is also worth noting that it was quickly cancelled.) On the other hand, could we create a series about the trials and tribulations of a loan officer where one episode involves a bank robbery? Sure. But the requirements of the on-going storylines would lead us to a very different approach to the subject matter, making the original concept unrecognizable.

Branding: The final consideration in television is the major difference in the diversity of programming on television and the "branding" of cable channels, networks, and streaming services.

Currently, there are only six major movie studios (possibly to become five by the time you read this as Disney is attempting to purchase Fox) that will buy a pitch and about the same number of mini-majors that are willing to develop this way. And many of these mini-majors end up distributing their product through one of the six major studios. Because of this, there are only a handful of people deciding what Hollywood movies get made. This leads to a fairly heterogeneous offering of product in the motion picture marketplace. By and large, all the studios will make comedies, action films, horror films, teen comedies, science fiction epics, and so on.

By comparison, there are dozens of networks, streaming services, cable channels, and production companies that develop scripted (and reality) programming. This diversity of choice in the television marketplace has led cable companies and networks to try to distinguish their programming in ways that are referred to as "branding." This is what leads the identity and style of a series programmed on AMC to be different from a series on NBC, The Disney Channel, and so on. From there you will need to drill down even further to the specific style of content and demographics that one channel serves versus another. These latter stylistic differences explain why "The Vampire Diaries" was programmed on The CW while "True Blood" was programmed on HBO. Both series involve vampires, but each series would never be programmed on the other channel. "True Blood" is able to delve into more explicit sex and violence because they are not bound by broadcast standards – and HBO can only win subscribers by programming material that cannot be found on broadcast television. "It's not TV. It's HBO," as they used to say.

Often, a network or cable channel's branded identity, as well as their "standards and practices," will dictate aspects of tone and content. Needless to say, they don't make anything like R-rated comedies on the Hallmark Channel. And while "The Walking Dead" is an indulgently violent series, the gruesome violence is only portrayed on the "walkers," and you will usually hear only a few four-letter words per show. In general, the economics of the broadcast networks, as well as the FCC obligations they have just by *being* broadcast networks, requires them to attract mass audiences. As a result, the shows they produce tend to be mostly inoffensive in the hopes of attracting the most viewers. On the other hand, the smaller "niche" cable channel may be looking to "make noise" by being provocative and therefore might actually *avoid* projects that feel too mainstream. This is another example of why a pitch needs to be matched with the right potential buyer.

The important point here is that an experienced television writer will almost always conceive of their television story with a handful of specific networks or cable companies in mind. If you come up with an idea for television and can't explain who would program it and why, pick another idea.

"HELL ON WHEELS"
by Tony Gayton

This whole thing started when my brother, Joe Gayton, and I were given a blind script deal at the production company Endemol. At the time, they were known mainly for reality shows like Big Brother but were looking to get into scripted shows. Joe and I put our heads together and came up with some ideas of our own, none of which were westerns. At this point, "Hell on Wheels," wasn't even a glimmer in our eyes.

We finally settled on an idea that everyone liked and worked out a pitch, which we took around town. The pitch was unceremoniously and unanimously rejected everywhere we went. It wasn't the first time that has happened and I'm sure it won't be the last (rejection can defeat you or inspire you – it's your choice).

Endemol informed us that even though AMC had passed on the pitch, they really wanted to find something else for us. They wondered if we would we be interested in trying to come up with a western-themed idea. Showing old western features and TV series is a big staple of AMC programming, so it made sense for them to want an original western series of their own.

I immediately remembered a documentary I had seen years before about the building of the transcontinental railroad. I remembered it was an epic American story and thought it would make a great TV series. It was just a matter of taking this gigantic story and coming up with a containable pitch. In hindsight, our pitch was still too big (we covered both the Union Pacific and the Central Pacific in our pitch) but I don't think that was a mistake. You will have plenty of time to winnow your show into something produce-able, but at the pitch stage, it's okay to go bigger if that helps you sell it.

We took a few weeks to nail down the pitch, before we pitched it to AMC. If memory serves, they bought it right away or damn near right away. The big lesson here is to know the needs of a network before you go out and pitch. There were only a limited number of places that would even touch a western. Some ideas will work for a broader spectrum of networks but some ideas will only be feasible at three or four places. The good news is that there are more and more cable channels sprouting up every day, so the number of homes for your ideas continues to increase.

The X-Factor.

There's an X-factor when it comes to picking a subject matter for a pitch, one that's harder to convey. You need to choose a story that is in sync with both your reputation and profile as a filmmaker and also in sync with the cultural climate of Hollywood.

Regarding a subject in sync with your profile as a writer or director, the simplest example is this: if you've only written or directed comedies, think twice before pitching a drama. And vice versa. This has to do with managing your career and what a buyer might reasonably be comfortable with you pitching. This doesn't mean you can't write a thriller if you've only ever written a drama. But before you can sell a thriller pitch, the buyer will probably want to see a sample of your work that's in the ballpark of a thriller. Look at your pitch meetings as a way to extend or enhance the value of your existing identity, or "brand," as an artist. As such, every pitch meeting is a special opportunity in your career. Don't squander the moment by pitching something where the buyer might reasonably question your ability to execute it.

As for getting in sync with Hollywood's cultural climate, showbiz has a reputation for being both liberal and also politically correct. There's no doubt that people in the Hollywood creative community slant to the political left, but above all else, Hollywood wants to make money. In practice this means that Hollywood shies away from subject matters that they feel might alienate a significant percentage of the audience. For example, if you plan to pitch a bio-film about the President being a spy for Russia, or an adaptation of Richard Dawkins' "The God Delusion," well, good luck with that. If the buyers think you are a kook, or someone with an axe to grind, don't be surprised if you don't sell a lot of pitches. Screenwriter Gary Goldman ("Total Recall," "Minority Report") puts it this way, "You're in the room to serve the marketplace. But it's also a pretty big marketplace. Try to find the sweet spot where your passions overlap with what Hollywood wants to make."

Ultimately, the X-factor has to do with how you want to present yourself as an artist to the Hollywood community.

Here is the bottom line. Take yourself and your pitch seriously and pick your subject matters shrewdly.

UNDERSTANDING YOUR CONCEPT

> *If you want a happy ending, that depends, of course, on where you stop your story.*
> —Orson Welles

Now that you've selected your subject matter, you will need to develop it into a pitch. It's possible that you've already begun to do so based on some of the guidelines we've given you. Or maybe you have a completed screenplay and you want to craft a compelling pitch so you can convince someone to read it. In the next chapter we will take you through the steps required to build a coherent and compelling pitch. But before we get there, we need to make sure you have a firm grasp of the two central elements of a pitch: *hook* and *character*. These two things deserve their own chapter because of the challenges they present for most people new to pitching.

We call this chapter "Understanding Your Concept" because, frankly, you'd be amazed how often we hear pitches where it is clear to us that the person pitching doesn't have a grasp of their own idea. In other words, they either haven't identified a compelling hook and character in their story, or maybe they've identified both elements but didn't actually deliver them in their pitch. When this latter thing happens, we sometimes (alliteratively) say that the pitch "didn't deliver on the *promise* of the *premise*." For example, imagine if you were pitching "Liar Liar" – a film about a lawyer who becomes a better man and father when he's cursed to tell the truth for a day – and half way through your pitch, it becomes a story that involves the CIA kidnaping the lawyer so they can learn how to make a better truth serum. Suddenly, your pitch becomes about something entirely different than the story promised by your concept or log line.

A related problem can arise when crafting a pitch to sell an already completed screenplay. The problem sometimes occurs because the writer has lost sight of their original hook and characters over the course of multiple drafts. Other times the person crafting the pitch gets lost in the sea of story details in their completed script and can no longer identify or articulate these key aspects. A telltale sign of both these problems is when you've crafted a great pitch and you realize it doesn't reflect what the script is actually about. When this happens, it is sobering. This is why we always suggest you craft the pitch for your screenplay *before* you try to write it. The script should serve the hook and characters, and not the other way around.

Most writers start building their pitch by sketching out a short plot summary of the final product, suitable for a 15-minute pitch. The choice of what to include and what to leave out is determined by how much is needed to ensure the abbreviated plotline is logical, coherent, and emphasizes the significant plot points of the story – the "plot mechanics." Almost all beginning writers are capable of this step, but this is also where most beginners get in trouble. This is most likely the result of a fundamental misunderstanding about what a pitch really is, and what the buyers are hoping to hear when they listen to a pitch.

Here's the fundamental problem:

While plot mechanics are usually the way a writer starts building a pitch, plot mechanics can be the enemy when it comes to actually pitching. The problem occurs because writers instinctively tend to pitch plot to show the buyer that they've "got it all worked out."

But plot isn't what sells your story in a pitch. Simply pitching, "X happens, then Y happens, then Z happens" isn't very compelling. This is an especially big challenge in more plot-driven genres such as mysteries or thrillers. And while the buyers want to know you have your plot all worked out, this is really not what they will be looking for when you pitch.

So, if making your pitch based on plotting is a mistake, what's the solution?

Focus on the hook and character. Before you can develop a compelling pitch, you need to identify these two elements. Usually, these two things are related but we will look at them individually.

The Hook.

As we said earlier, a hook refers to the element of the story's concept that amplifies the stakes and compels our interest (the term comes from the idea of a fish hook – it's what catches the audience's attention). For example, in the 1997 film "Liar Liar," Jim Carrey plays a lawyer cursed to tell the truth for 24 hours – a great and intriguing hook, considering that most people assume lawyers lie for a living. But it's not the plot details of the trial that compel our interest in the film (does anyone even remember the court case?), but rather how the character's curse complicates and thwarts him from getting the things *he wants* in the story: reconciling with his son and being the better father that he wants to be. Would "Liar Liar" have had the same hook if the lead were a doctor? Probably not. An accountant? Not unless he's an accountant for the Mafia, where the stakes might be life or death. A politician? Maybe. If you understand the implication of the differences here, you will start to understand how learning to pitch can help you access the most compelling version of your idea.

Most of your pitch should focus on the hook of the idea, no matter how detailed the plot summary. Continuing with "Liar Liar" as our example, you would focus on what happens when someone who lies for a living is forced to tell the truth for 24 hours. And the part of your pitch that doesn't focus on dramatizing the hook will likely involve *setting up* the hook, probably in the first act of the story. In fact, this is one of the central things that the set-up of a pitch (or a script, for that matter) is supposed to be setting up!

There's an old joke in biology that a chicken is an egg's way of producing another *egg*. The joke is meant to illustrate the primacy of DNA (contained in the egg) in the circle of life. Using this comparison, the hook is your story's DNA. The plot (like the chicken) is the thing that's there to propagate your hook. A pitch that doesn't keep its core hook front and center is a pitch that is not playing to its strengths.

In most pitching situations, the buyer will be listening closely, attempting to identify the hook in your story. There are several reasons for this. First of all, understanding the hook will probably inform the buyer of how they will sell your project in the marketplace after your project gets made. With millions of dollars on the line, this is a critical judgment.

Secondly, it's likely that the person hearing your pitch will subsequently have to present the pitch to their boss. When this happens, it's unlikely the person will be able to recount every beat of the story you told them. So, what are they re-pitching? That's right: character and hook.

Lastly, as a generalization, buyers prefer a pitch with a good concept (character and hook) to one without these qualities, but that is otherwise well told. This is not to say that a well-told story has no value. It does. A good story is a good story and it would be a mistake to think that buyers are all philistines, as they are often portrayed. But when given the choice, most buyers will prefer an idea with a great hook to an idea with a weaker hook if the latter one's success is dependent on a brilliantly written script to be viable in the marketplace. These latter ideas are called "execution-dependent." If the studio buys a good idea and the writer fails in his or her execution, well, at least they still own a good idea that some other writer might be able to fix. If they buy a pitch with a weak idea that ends up as a poorly executed screenplay, they have nothing but dead trees. And the less experienced the writer, the less willing the buyer will be to gamble on their ability to execute. We should point out that this situation mostly applies to motion picture scripts. It is far less common in series television, where writers are rarely hired to rewrite another writer's original pilot, no matter how great the idea. We will discuss why this is in our chapter about pitching for television.

Character.

The presentation of character in pitching is just as important. And, of course, character is related to the hook. In the example of "Liar Liar," we are interested in the story because we want to find out what happens to the lawyer with a curse. The hook isn't just an intellectual gimmick; it is something that happens to a character we care about. Now, let's consider the character's place in a pitch.

After losing the hook, the biggest mistake a screenwriter can make when pitching is to lose their characters' presence in all the plot machinations. We don't mean that the characters don't appear in the plot, but rather that the characters become secondary to the plot, like chess pieces, taking action without emotional impact.

Character is our way into a story. We care about the outcome of the plot because we care what happens to one or more characters caught up in it. In "Liar Liar" we care about the lawyer – even though he is actually kind of a jerk in the beginning – because we see that he has a son – a good kid who needs a better relationship with his dad. His dad recognizes this and wants to be better for his son. We are rooting for the lawyer to change. This is why the hook matters – being forced to tell the truth could make the hero a better father. The goal of pitching (and writing, for that matter) is to dramatize this aspect of the hook and not let your pitch degenerate into a series of meaningless plot points.

A successful pitch will make the buyer care about the characters and show how the plot twists affect them. It might be more accurate to say that, while plot can be presented in a pitch in some detail, it is always best if plot is presented in the *context* of character. We'll do two different versions of a short excerpt from a hypothetical pitch for "Liar Liar" so our meaning is clear.

"Fletcher has to figure out how to win the case without lying. But it turns out Samantha has lied about her age and was a minor when she signed the pre-nup, thus rendering it invalid. Fletcher presents this evidence in court and the judge awards custody of the kids to Samantha. But Fletcher realizes she's only using the kids to get more money from her ex. Fletcher demands that the judge reverse his decision. The judge refuses and Fletcher is arrested for contempt of court."

Plot driven and uninvolving. Try this instead:

"With his career on the line, Fletcher is desperate to figure out a way to win his case without lying. And when he discovers Samantha lied about her age – she was a minor when she signed the pre-nup, he's overjoyed! The document is invalid. He can win his case despite the curse. But when he watches Samantha rip the children from the arms of their loving father, Fletcher's joy fades. He now knows Samantha was just using the kids for the money. Fletcher thinks of his own son, Max, and knows he must do the right thing. He begs that the judge reverse the decision. But the judge refuses and Fletcher is arrested for contempt of court."

In this second example the same action occurs but ever-present are Fletcher's motivation, his action-reaction and the emotional impact of the events. Or generically, the character did X, which caused Y to happen, which affected the character, so the character did Z.

What the buyers are looking for is an interesting idea (strong concept with a good hook) that gets their attention, and a relatable character that goes on a powerful emotional journey. Buyers are only concerned with the events of the plot insomuch as they support this journey. Let's analyze the hook and character for our heist film idea.

Hook: While bank robberies are a staple of Hollywood movies and television shows, a bank robbery in and of itself does not create the hook for our idea. We've seen it a thousand times. What is different about our story is the quadriplegic mastermind villain. Of course we're faced with a problem – we want the fact that this character is a villain to be a twist. This means that we will often not be able to use it to create initial intrigue. But perhaps we can use the fact that our apparent heroes are a mild-mannered bank manager and a quadriplegic, two people unlikely to save hostages from bank robbers! That's intriguing, and it illustrates our point that what is most interesting about a story concept is often found in character rather than plot.

Character: Our hero is John, a loan officer in a bank. We will care about John because he is exceptionally compassionate, helpful and self-sacrificing. He will also end up risking his own life to help others. This will require him to change – the "character arc" – from mild-mannered to action hero. We also have Tony, the quadriplegic, who – in a plot twist – will turn out to be the villain. As we develop the pitch we will want to keep these elements – John's arc on his journey to Tony's betrayal – front and center.

One last note before we move on: If you're trying to develop your pitch based on an existing script, you may discover that the most compelling version of your idea is *not* embodied in your script. This is another example of how learning to pitch can help you uncover the DNA of your idea. And this is why we recommend that most writers envision the pitch for their script *before* they write it. Unfortunately, this is almost never how writers work.

If you find yourself in this situation, we encourage you to go back and revise your script and conform it to your newly discovered DNA. The result will be a better and more marketable screenplay.

"THE GREAT DEBATERS"

by Robert Eisele

The project began when my old college friend, Jeff Porro, sent me an article from the African-American history magazine, American Legacy, entitled "The Great Debaters."

The article summarized a triumphant period in the 1930s when a black college debate team – Wiley College of Marshall, Texas – became the first African-American school to debate white colleges and universities in the Deep South. Wiley College's debaters remained undefeated for years, and even beat the national champs. For over a decade, Professor Melvin Tolson, the team's coach, challenged racial segregation with the debate teams he trained. What a great subject for a powerful, inspirational film. I was hooked immediately.

Jeff and I decided to option the article and collaborate on the story. Since I was the professional screenwriter (Jeff is a speech writer in Washington, D.C.), we agreed I would write the script solo if we sold the idea. So I started developing the pitch.

The source material presented several challenges.

First of all, the article encompassed ten years of history, a focus too broad for a feature film pitch. So we researched the subject thoroughly, interviewed the few surviving members of the debate team, and identified a viable time frame.

We decided to focus our pitch on the 1935 season, the year Wiley beat the national champs. Every story needs a great villain and ours was Jim Crow – racial segregation itself. On a deeper level, the antagonist was the self-doubt that discrimination engendered, even in these gifted college students. While a story set at a black college in the 1930s might seem un-commercial, I knew there was a powerful theme here – the triumph of the human spirit. And the struggle of the underdog defying all odds has universal appeal. Inspirational dramas like "The Great Debaters" can get made in Hollywood if they're done right, but they must be compelling and fully realized.

I also knew my pitch would appeal to producers with a social conscience – those looking for stories that portray African-Americans in a positive light. With that in mind, my agents advised us to pitch the idea to Harpo, Oprah Winfrey's company. The creative execs at Harpo loved it, and soon we had a pitch meeting set at Miramax.

At the time, Miramax was known for their risk-taking with challenging subject matters. We pitched the story to the execs there and they bought it, paying me to write the script. Choosing the right buyer is as important as creating a good pitch.

Soon after, Denzel Washington read the script, loved it, and decided to direct it. In 2007, "The Great Debaters" finally made it to the screen.

The movie was a 2008 Golden Globe Best Picture nominee and won numerous awards, among them the Writers Guild of America's Paul Selvin Award, the Image Award for Best Picture, and the Producers Guild Stanley Kramer Award.

LET'S CREATE A PITCH

> "A good film is when the price of the dinner, the theatre admission and the babysitter were worth it."
> —Alfred Hitchcock

Once you've chosen appropriate subject matter and developed the concept, the next step is constructing your pitch. As we've said, this isn't a book about screenwriting, so we will assume you have already developed a complete, dramatic, compelling story.

There will be situations where you will be required to pitch your story in a time frame that ranges from 15 seconds (your log line) up to 15 minutes (20 minutes is considered the unofficial upper limit). What follows is a detailed description of how you build a full-length feature film pitch. Later on, we will show you how to build shorter versions. We will also give you several examples of pitches of different length so you can see how the complex elements of a pitch are put into practice. You will see how pitches that run between 2 minutes and 15 minutes share similar elements but in different proportions. The key is the different *intentions* of the different length pitches, and this is what determines the relative balance of the respective elements. You can probably guess that a longer pitch will convey more plot than a shorter pitch, and you'd be correct. The real question is why plot is more important in the longer pitch – which we will get to in a bit.

The sequence of steps for pitches that run about 2 minutes or longer are as follows, and they are pitched, with few exceptions, in this order:

1. Personal Connection
2. Rating/Genre/Tone
3. Title (sometimes optional)
4. Log Line
5. The Unique World or Rules (if needed)
6. Introduce Your Main Characters
7. The Story (or story set-up, in a shorter pitch)

These are the essential elements required so that you pitch has the best chance of communicating what you intend. Sounds simple enough, right? Not really, and there are many factors to consider. But keep this outline in mind as we dig into the details so you don't lose sight of the big picture. Remember, these are the steps for a motion picture pitch. There will be overlap with a television pitch.

Personal Connection.

The most effective way to start your pitch is by establishing your "personal connection" to the project you are pitching. A personal connection is the way a writer, director, or producer builds the foundation for the project they are about to pitch. We call it "personal" because it can convey how the project originated with you, your unique reason for wanting to tell this particular story, why you think it deserves to be told, and/or why you are uniquely qualified to tell it. A pitch is as much about selling your credibility as an artist as it is about selling the project, and the personal connection is where the case is made for your participation. This doesn't mean that your personal connection must be an autobiographical story, though it could be.

Establishing a good personal connection is one of the most important and difficult pitching skills to master. This is because there are as many possible personal connections as there are filmmakers and stories, and because the personal connection can accomplish so many different (and difficult) things in a pitch, including:

- It eases the listener into your pitch as you transition from the small talk at the start of a meeting, helping you set the stage for the story to follow.
- It establishes your connection to the story (if it's an original idea), or your unique point of view (if it's not original). If you're a writer or director, this will imply why you are the best person for the job.
- A personal connection can explain why your story matters and why it will matter to the audience. In other words, it establishes why this story ought to be told. In this regard it is a marketing tool for your idea.
- A personal connection can establish the emotional or thematic core of your story – it's "heart" – in a way that is much harder to accomplish later in a pitch.
- It can create intrigue, piquing the listener's curiosity and whetting their appetite for your idea.

Several of these are complex notions, and in a shorter pitch it's not unusual for the personal connection to take up a significant percentage of the total time. You should take that as a reflection of how important the personal connection can be to selling your project. We often joke that most pitches are sold in the first two minutes – and you hope the rest of the pitch just doesn't screw it up. The personal connection does much of the heavy lifting in selling a pitch. When it's done right, all these components of a personal connection are interrelated and flow seamlessly from one into another. Let's examine the above aspects of a personal connection in a little more detail.

Ease the Listener: There's a point in most pitch meetings where the conversation turns from small talk about the weather and where you're from to business. We touch upon this topic later when we discuss meeting etiquette, but very often the listener will cue you that it's time to pitch by saying something like, "So what are you working on?" or "What did you think of the book we sent you?" Using the personal connection to gracefully segue to your pitch keeps things conversational. You might start by saying something like, "I'm working on a horror idea. When I was a kid, I was terrified of clowns…"

If the listener doesn't segue from small talk quickly enough, you can spur the conversation in that direction. Remember, your pitch is most likely the main reason for the meeting. You want to make sure you give it adequate time.

Example:

"Well, I know you are busy, so let me get to the reason I'm here today. I am so excited to have a chance to talk to you about a story based on something that happened to me the other day in a bank…"

Or, if it's a rewrite:

"Thanks for sending me the script. It's a great project. My mom was a bank teller, so it brought back a lot of memories."

When crafting your personal connection, you want to make it conversational. You don't want to say something like, "My personal connection to the material is…" That will come off as stilted and awkward. Rather, imagine you are telling a friend how you came up with the idea for your latest project.

Establish Your Connection: If you're pitching an original idea, you should try to establish the genesis of the idea. We don't mean, "I was in the bathtub and so had time to think" – we are not necessarily referring to *where* you were when you got the idea (although it is possible that could be a plus) – we are talking about inspiration. This is more than just saying, "I played with trains when I was a kid, and so I'd like to do a film set on a train." The origin of your idea should be related to why your idea is fresh and/or compelling, i.e. your hook. Also, buyers want to know that you are inspired by the project because that means you are likely to do your best work.

If you're pitching an adaptation, or a rewrite assignment, or something you didn't create, the connection becomes a little different. This would also be the case if, for example, you are a director trying to get hired on a film or television project. Here is where we add the "personal" in personal connection. You have to explain 1) why you liked the existing material, 2) why it spoke to you on some fundamental level, and by inference, 3) why you are the best person for the job. If you were adept at explaining the first two, the last one will be obvious to your listener.

As writer/director Eric Heisserer ("Arrival," "Lights Out") says, "I've come to realize I can't pitch on something unless I have a personal, emotional connection to it somehow. A story from my own youth. A main character drawn from my father or in-law. An event that changed my life or the life of a loved one. It's critical your audience understands where your heart is with the story, they don't want it to be merely business. Or to put it this way: If two writers come in and pitch, and both takes are competent, the one who demonstrates why it matters to them or how it's based on a personal story will get the job, because it suggests the material will be written with passion and emotional drive otherwise missing from the other take."

A note of caution: one of the biggest mistakes you can make with the personal connection (other than not having one) is lack of focus. For example, the significance of a story's origins can usually be explained in a few sentences. Rambling on for five minutes will not make it any more fascinating to your listener. They don't want to hear your life story, unless you are pitching your life story. Make it short and to the point and make clear what aspect you want your listener to pull from your origins story. The goal is to serve the pitch to come, so make sure the connection is relevant, specific and clear.

Using our heist example:

"I'm a big fan of Stephen Hawking. It's hard to imagine what it must have been like for him, growing up, being so much smarter than nearly everyone around him – and what it must have been like for someone so brilliant to lose all mobility. How does someone like that stay positive? And what if he hadn't? What if instead he became twisted and used his amazing mind for evil? What if he became a criminal? With his intelligence and unthreatening appearance, he could get away with anything! And that gave me an idea for a heist movie with a disabled criminal mastermind, someone most people pity, but is in fact the most dangerous man in the room. After all, it's the memorable villain that makes a heist movie great."

Notice how our example concisely connects three things: where the idea originated (fan of Stephen Hawking), what was memorable about it (he would be an unlikely villain), and what will be exciting about the story (a bank heist). You might also notice that the thing that makes this personal connection "personal" is our speculation into an alternative way that a disability might have impacted the smartest guy in the world. It's less about our experiences and more about our unique perspective.

Why it Matters: This is the toughest aspect of a personal connection. You must make the case for why your project deserves to live in a crowded media marketplace. It's not a given that your listener will understand this based solely on your pitch. Strangely, the same challenge often applies when pitching to land an assignment where, presumably, the buyer already believes in the virtues of the project. But the reality is that buyers often have many projects, and they're always looking for inspired filmmakers help the narrow the buyer's field of choices. Explaining why this project matters is part of that process.

Many projects get pitched, few get bought, and vastly fewer get made, so your reasoning needs to be very, very compelling. If your only reason for pitching this idea were, "because the rent is due," your pitch will come off as cynical and you will fail to inspire the excitement needed to sell your idea.

Similarly, if your explanation for why you are pitching, say, a science fiction movie is generic, such as "kids like special effects," you're not digging deep enough. This is probably why so many people have trouble with this aspect of pitching. Making the case for why your idea, or point of view, is worthy of existing in a crowded marketplace is a daunting task, even for a seasoned pro. This is why we referred to this element of a personal connection as a "marketing tool."

Establish the Emotional or Thematic Core: This is a way of informing the listener about the heart of your project. It gives you an opportunity to identify these more meaningful aspects of the project so you don't have to do so in the story section of your pitch, where it will usually be considered pretentious. Keep in mind that establishing an emotional or thematic core does not relieve you of justifying its value. You might be passionate about a project that deals with "a man confronting a vast and indifferent universe," but why an audience will care about that theme is not a given! And, of course, the story you are about to pitch must *dramatize* this theme.

Continuing our example: "At its core I think this could be a fascinating story about a fundamentally good man in a dangerous situation. A man who sees the best in his fellow men and what happens when his human decency is betrayed? What kind of man will he become then?"

The personal connection allows you the opportunity to speak from your heart and let the listener know what the project *means* to you – again, it's *personal*.

Creating Intrigue: This is often related to why your idea is compelling in the first place, and it is pretty well expressed by the last sentence of the above example. We are teasing the listener, raising a question that will be answered by the story. This engages the listener – assuming, of course, the question raised is interesting. And hopefully it is obvious that whatever intrigue you establish in your personal connection must be fully realized or paid off later in the pitch. The intrigue should relate to a core element of your story.

* * *

Taken as a whole, you can see why mastering the above five functions of the personal connection can be so complex and why it is challenging to accomplish, even for a pro. Of course, a personal connection does *not* have to do all five of these things, and in a short pitch it would be ludicrous to try. But as you start to build your personal connection, try to answer the following two questions about your story:

1. What is my unique, authentic and compelling relationship to, or understanding of, the subject matter?

2. What aspect of my subject matter might need the most help to explain, or set up, before I launch into the body of my pitch?

Your personal connection may not be immediately obvious to you, but if you are passionate about the story – and you ought to be if you're pitching it – there must be some connection. What was the thing that compelled you to pitch or write it in the first place?

If you're pitching a story based on something that happened in your own life, great. Describe the real events that inspired you and why they were so meaningful. If you have a specialized expertise in the arena – you were a fireman and you're pitching a story about firemen, for example – then use that. But be certain to close the gap between your experience and the story. You do this by describing the insight your experience gave you that serves as the basis for your take on the idea.

Let's say you are a guy writing about your experiences working in a day care center in college. You could open your pitch by saying:

"In college, I worked in a day care center. There are so many hilarious things that happened there, I thought it would be a great setting for a romantic comedy between a teacher and a single mother."

Good, but not great. This example demonstrates that you have some expertise or experience that will provide authenticity and specificity to your story. But it doesn't really close the gap between your experience and the story you want to tell. A better opening would be to say:

"In college, I worked in a day care center. I was prepared for crazy kids, but what I wasn't prepared for was how all of the single mothers hit on me every day. Turns out a single guy who works with kids is catnip for moms. So I came up with a romantic comedy between a teacher and a parent."

There is a pitfall when describing a personal experience to open your pitch. You need to make sure that the story you relate is not going to make the listener too uncomfortable. If you are going to talk about some horrific experience you had, you have to do it in a way that doesn't make people squirm. This can be tricky, and sometimes you might want to avoid connections that are too personal.

Most of the time, though, you won't be pitching a story that's even semi-autobiographical. This means you'll have to dig deeper to show your connection. If it's an original story, you might say what inspired you to create it. Even though it's not autobiographical, perhaps you can describe how an experience gave you a unique insight into something familiar.

For example, you might say, "I just attended Spring Break in Florida and while everyone knows about the 'sex, drugs and rock 'n' roll,' I want to tell the story from the point of view of the dedicated EMTs who have to keep 25,000 fun-loving college kids alive for one week."

You may never have been an EMT, but still managed to find a unique perspective – based on your experiences – into a familiar subject matter.

Now imagine if you are pitching something far removed from the experiences of daily life. For example, if you are pitching fantasy, science fiction, or a historical piece, you might have a hard time connecting the story to a literal experience you've had. But hopefully there's some aspect of the concept or story that connects to common experiences of people living in the real world today. If not, why will anyone care about your idea?

Consider "Dunkirk," Christopher Nolan's 2017 hit film about the desperate evacuation of British troops just before the Nazi invasion of France in 1940. Nolan was never a solider, never fought in the war. And, on one level, the film is about a towering defeat. But Nolan remembered hearing stories of the events as a boy and was inspired to illuminate the *unexpected* acts of heroism and bravery of the soldiers and civilians amidst the messy chaos of retreat. This latter perspective was his personal connection, his unique insight into an otherwise familiar story.

Consider the 2017 hit movie "The Post," which was conceived by a first-time writer, Elizabeth Hannah. Hannah was too young to have lived through the events portrayed, and there were any number of ways she could have chosen to approach and dramatize the story. But she centered her story on a woman finding her voice in a male dominated industry – undoubtedly something a fledgling writer like Hannah could relate to personally.

Or look at "Star Wars" – George Lucas grew up in Modesto, California racing cars and dreaming of adventure. He *was* Luke Skywalker, even though he didn't live "a long time ago in a galaxy far, far away." This is a perfect example of connecting a story with an unfamiliar setting to something personal – grounding the story by telling something about yourself in a way that makes the story relevant. But again, be sure to connect the dots for the listener between your personal experiences and the story you are telling.

Simply having an interest in a subject is rarely enough to create the personal connection unless you can establish a special insight you have to the topic and create intrigue. For example, you might say, "I've always been interested in the Revolutionary War and I've read dozens of books about it. I was surprised to discover that George Washington was among the first military leaders in the world to embrace espionage. It was generally considered underhanded at the time. As a result, many of the spies he recruited had shady pasts. I thought it would be interesting to see how someone with a crooked past could be redeemed by serving the revolution."

Another approach is the, "What if..." personal connection. This is where you take something that interests you and propose an intriguing story twist on the subject. For example, "I read a fascinating article about all the skills needed to survive for a week in the wilderness. It made me wonder how many would apply to an urban environment. I thought, 'What if a wilderness survival expert is forced to survive on the mean streets of New York? How would he fare?'" A good example of this is the 2015 movie, "Spy," which asks what if you put a dowdy, meek woman at the center of a James Bond movie instead of a macho superspy? Or the series "The Man in the High Castle," which imagines what if the Germans and Japanese had won World War II and both occupied the United States? Or "The Purge," which asks what would happen if all laws were suspended one day a year.

* * *

As you can see, there are a lot of ways into a personal connection. There are also many pitfalls. We have seen writers craft a great personal connection, but then it doesn't actually pay off in the story. For example, if you say you were intrigued by the EMTs at Spring Break and your pitch is about a surgeon at the hospital with a drug problem, you are not really connecting your personal insight with the story you actually tell. In such a case, your personal connection does none of the "heavy lifting" a personal connection can accomplish when it's done right!

Sometimes, your personal connection hints at the emotion embedded in your concept – as saving kids' lives does in the Spring Break story, for example. If the story you tell doesn't deliver on those emotions, you are failing to live up to the promise of your personal connection.

In our romantic comedy idea set in a day care center, the implication of the personal connection is that the lead will be a young man who finds himself an object of desire for multiple women. We would expect this young man would learn something about love and commitment from such an experience. If the story were actually about a young man learning responsibility, a personal connection about amorous single mothers is probably not the best approach. Instead, you might want to say something like: "In college I worked in a day care center, which was ironic because I wasn't much more mature than the five-year-olds put under my care. But when one troubled young boy came to the center, it really pushed me to think about the impact adults have on children. Working with that boy caused me to grow up."

Any pitch over 30 seconds will benefit from a personal connection, even if it's just a couple of clever sentences. The amount of time you spend on this aspect will vary depending on the length of the pitch and how much set up your pitch requires. But remember that the personal connection is just the set-up, not the story. Don't belabor it with unnecessary detail.

Genre, Rating and Tone.

At the most basic level, the pitch is a verbal summary of your story. But it is actually more than that – you are trying to convey the experience of the movie you want to create. While some aspects of the experience can be conveyed in the body of your story, many others cannot. So before launching into the bulk of your pitch, you need to establish what kind of movie you're envisioning. This usually includes the tone, genre and rating. While these elements should be obvious when you read a well-executed screenplay, they are much harder to convey verbally in a pitch.

As we mentioned earlier, this is one of the most fundamental ways your project will be categorized. Don't make the listener guess if it's a comedy or not, or if it will be R or PG. It's okay to say, "This is a sexy romantic comedy," or, "This is a graphic, R-rated horror movie." It helps the listener contextualize the story you are about to describe. Of course, you should also make sure that what you establish here is reflected in the pitch itself. As we said before, a comedy pitch that is not funny, or a romance that doesn't tug at the heartstrings, or a horror pitch that doesn't bring the terror are all almost surely doomed to fail. (If you are pitching a television project, there is no need to mention the MPAA rating.) Often, the genre and rating will be incorporated into the log line, typically in the first half of the *first* sentence. As we said earlier, the description of genres is a cultural thing in Hollywood and there is a partial list of traditional examples at the end of this book.

The Title.

Naturally, if you're pitching an assignment or adaptation it's likely the listener will already know the title, but if you're pitching an original idea, have a good title for it. It helps make the movie seem real. Make sure the reason for your title is clear. It doesn't help your pitch if the title is abstract or seemingly unrelated to the subject matter. A good title is one that helps sell the idea by amplifying some aspect of the idea. "Gravity" is an example of a good title because it conveys two aspects that are relevant to the story: the lack of weight in space, and the dire nature of the story. Using our heist story as an example, "The Hostage" would be a much better title choice than, say, calling it "The Fishbowl," unless (for example) our pitch uses a fishbowl as a clear metaphor or a fishbowl is used as a significant prop in the story.

The Log Line.

Next, you will want to frame your story by giving a log line.

The ability to create a great log line is a valuable skill in Hollywood, but it's also a complex and tricky task. A good log line will help convey the gist of the idea you are about to pitch in a way that is succinct and compelling. This is important because it is easy for a listener to get lost in the sea of detail that will follow, and a solid log line will help the listener process the information. Once they know the concept (as conveyed in the log line) of your film, they can sit back and enjoy the character and plot elements you present and (ideally) understand how they fit into the big picture. The log line becomes the framework (or "road map") for the listener from which you hang the rest of the pitch.

To illustrate this point, imagine you asked someone to tell you everywhere they went this morning. (Why you would do such a thing, we have no idea.) They might start by saying:

I left my home and headed east on Moorpark Ave.
I drove for about half a mile, then made a left on Woodman Avenue.
I took Woodman for about a quarter mile until I saw the sign that said US101 South.
I got on the freeway going south. I was lucky; traffic was light.
A short time later, I saw the sign that said CA134 East and got in the left lane so I didn't miss the exit.

And so on…

Have you lost consciousness yet? Pretty tedious, right?

Now imagine instead that they had just said this:

I drove to ArtCenter College of Design in Pasadena, California. To get there, I left my home and headed east on Moorpark Ave. I drove for about half a mile, then made a left on Woodman Avenue.

And so on. Better, right?

Do you see how these two versions are really the same story? Notice how the latter version summarizes the trip, and the intended destination, in a way that is both brief and clear. Before the speaker takes you through the trip step by step, you know where they are headed so their driving choices have context.

The overwhelming number of pitches you will make in your career will be of the "stand-alone," 15-second variety, which is another way of saying a "one-liner" or log line. We say stand-alone because a log line is *also* a component of a longer pitch, as we are now describing. But most often, you will be asked to deliver the shortest version of your idea when responding to the ubiquitous question from a very busy person, "So, what's it about?" And even though ideas are not really sold in 15 seconds, you want to make sure you have a good answer for this question when it comes. The time to figure out the answer to that question is *not* when you are asked. Don't try to reach for it in the moment. Based on experience, we know that most people – even the pros – struggle with creating a good log line, even when they have plenty of lead-time. Very, very few people can rattle off a good log line extemporaneously.

For something so brief, creating a good log line is much harder than it seems. It requires precision of language and a good dose of narrative insight. Precision, because when you are working with 25 to 50 words, your choice of every word must be exacting. Narrative insight, because picking the right words requires that you fully understand what aspects of a concept (and story) are the essentially appealing ones. But when it's done right, a good log line is a thing of beauty – like poetry – as dynamic as it is economical. The good news is that the formal aspects of crafting a good log line can be learned.

Earlier we mentioned that the ideal log line is also high-concept, but not all log lines are high-concept any more than all film or television projects are high-concept. Still, the goal of a good log line is similar to the goal of high-concept: to create a short summary that is as succinct and compelling as possible. Usually, the more high-concept the idea, the shorter the log line can be. A 3-sentence description is considered the upper limit for a log line for a complex story idea. Keep in mind that the demands of stand-alone log lines can be a little different than a log line used in the context of a longer pitch (as we are discussing in this section of the book). If you're only doing a stand-alone log line, it might have to work a little harder to sell your story idea. We will start by talking about stand-alone log lines because they are the most complete version.

Typically, a stand-alone log line will contain the following elements, and more or less in this order:

- Title/Rating/Genre
- Establish an unfamiliar setting
- Identify your protagonist
- Identify your protagonist's goal
- Identify the antagonist
- Set up the story

Now let's explore each of these in more detail.

Title/Rating/Genre. Most stand-alone log lines for movies will lead with the rating and genre just as those aspects are included in a longer pitch: A PG-13 action/thriller, an R-rated comedy, a PG animated adventure, etc. You don't always need to give a title, but if you have a good one, it can be included here as well. If your title's meaning is oblique, leave it out of your stand-alone log line. To be clear, the rating is used as a proxy for your listener in a pitch to someone in the business. If you are drafting a log line for, say, a film festival catalog, and your film has not been rated by the MPAA, you would omit the rating.

Establishing an Unfamiliar Setting. If the setting of your story is unfamiliar or will not be obvious or clear in the body of your log line, you should establish it up front. This is frequently a requirement with historical, science fiction or fantasy subject matters, but there are many other unfamiliar settings portrayed in film and television where the environment, and/or the rules of the world, needs to be established. For example, try to imagine how difficult it would be to describe the unique worlds of the "Hobbit" or "The Lord of the Rings" in a short phrase if the books did not exist. It would be formidable, but maybe not impossible. You might describe it as set "in a fantasy medieval world of magic and monsters." That might be close enough for the purpose of a log line. There are also many real-world settings that will require some set up. The unique worlds of "Molly's Game," "The Fast and the Furious" and "The Godfather," are all good examples. You could say "Molly's Game" is "set inside the high-stakes world of elite private poker games" and "The Fast and the Furious" is "set in the exciting sub-culture of illegal street-racing." It is crucial that you paint a vivid picture in the mind of the listener of your unfamiliar setting. If you don't, it is likely they will struggle to understand everything that follows.

Identify Your Protagonist. Who is the protagonist? In other words, through whose point of view is the listener experiencing the events of the story? Try to identify the primary aspects of the protagonist that matter for your log line. Referring to the protagonist merely as a "man" or a "woman" is almost never enough. It is often better to identify the protagonist by what they do. Is he or she a cop, a superhero, a doctor, a mother? But make sure your description is relevant to what comes later in your log line! In other words, if you describe your lead as a cop, and what follows is not a story that involves cop-things, there might be a better way to describe the lead. One other important thing – if your lead is under 18, specify the age exactly. Calling someone a child or kid is vague. There's a big difference between a 5-year-old and a 12-year-old. Otherwise, you probably won't specify the character's age in the log line unless their exact age is important to the story – for example, a story about a character's first trip to Las Vegas at 21, or forced retirement at 65, etc.

Usually, the earlier you can identify your protagonist in your log line the better. So, "A resourceful scientist fights back when the Earth is attacked by aliens" is better than, "After the Earth is attacked by aliens, a resourceful scientist tries to fight back." Do you see how the first version keeps the primary focus on the lead? (If the aliens are the stars of this film – never mind.) You want your protagonist at the center of your story's reason to exist.

You don't need to give your protagonist a name. Proper nouns convey very little information in most log lines. You should only give your protagonist a name in a short log line if they are based on a famous fictional, mythical or real-life person – in other words, if your listener will recognize the name when they hear it. If your character's name is something like, Harry Potter, Dracula, Noah, Santa Claus or George Washington, by all means let your listener know! This is a marketing decision.

If your story is about a group, or a team (sometimes referred to as an "ensemble") – try to characterize the group. "A team of superheroes," "a dysfunctional family," or a "motley band of soldiers," are all good examples. This usually applies if there are more than two central characters. If you were doing a story with two equal leads, such as a romance or a buddy story, each character would more likely be described individually. For example, "Notting Hill" would probably be described as a romance between a "British bookseller and an American movie star." A typical exception would be for a comedy like "This is 40," where the two protagonists might be collectively described as a "middle-aged, married couple." Of course, some romances and buddy films have more than two leads, such as "Love Actually" or "Bad Moms," respectively. In films like these, you will need to summarize the group in some way – "A cross section of lovelorn Londoners" or "Three stressed-out, suburban mothers."

One last aspect of establishing your protagonist is the use of adjectives to enhance the description of them. You may have noticed how we slipped this into the last two examples. ("Lovelorn" and "stressed-out.") In most cases, you should choose an adjective that will help the listener zero in on the protagonist's primary quality: "a *lonely* housewife," "a *reluctant* superhero," "a *dysfunctional* family," and so on.

Adjectives can be a log line's best friend if done right. Two tips for doing it right:

First, try to choose an adjective that confers a dramatic, dynamic, sympathetic, or admirable quality to your protagonist. You're describing your lead, after all. This doesn't mean your choice has to imply heroism or perfection. Flawed characters are okay, but there's a huge difference between describing them as a "loser" versus "down on their luck." The latter is much more sympathetic. Remember, the listener does not have the benefit of knowing all the complexity of your character that will appear in the screenplay. They will build their impression entirely on what words you use to describe them here.

Second, your choice of adjective *must* be relevant to the events or actions that follow in your log line. This is very important. So, a *lonely* housewife *finds* true love, a *reluctant* superhero *rediscovers* his courage, and a *dysfunctional* family *learns to live* together. Do you see how these character descriptions and actions that follow complement and are in sync with each other?

One last piece of advice: it is very easy to slip into some bad clichés with adjectives if you're not artful. Some of the examples above come pretty close, but we chose them just for clarity. Use a thesaurus; find the best words, ones that are both fresh and evocative.

Protagonist's Goal. Once we identify the protagonist, next we must articulate their main goal for the bulk of the story. What do they really want? So, for example, in the movie "Gravity," the astronaut's main goal is to survive a disaster and return to Earth.

It's not to repair the Hubble Telescope, although that is her initial goal. This is a crucial distinction. You must identify what drives the drama for most of your story. If your log line is for a movie, the protagonist's goal should be the thing that drives the story for perhaps 90 minutes of screen time. If it's a television series log line, it might have to help drive the stories of 60 episodes, or more! In almost all cases, the protagonist's goal will be described with a verb – "survive" and "return," in our "Gravity" example above.

Be careful when selecting the appropriate verb. Make sure it describes something that can be ongoing and sustained. This too is very important. Stay away from verbs that imply very transient things for the protagonist. Verbs like "discovers" or "realizes" or "decides" imply a very brief screen time, unless followed up with another verb that describes the protagonist's actions after that discovery, realization or decision! It only takes a few minutes of screen time for the astronaut in "Gravity" to *discover* her space shuttle has been destroyed, but it takes the rest of the film for her to *survive* and *return* to Earth, so the latter is an example of what you want to capture in your log line. Also, look for external, visual verbs. If you say your character "contemplates" something, the listener might imagine a movie of someone looking out the window pensively. Remember, film is a visual medium.

If you're having a hard time identifying your protagonist's goal, it is probably a good indication that your story has some fundamental flaw. Once again, this is an example of how pitching can be a tool that helps you uncover the DNA of your story and make it better. This is a core principle of this book.

Identify the Antagonist. Directly related to the protagonist's goal is the thing that prevents him or her from attaining it. You'll want to make it clear who or what that is. This is your antagonist. Notice we said who or *what*. In many cases, there is no who. In the case of "Gravity," the antagonist is the deadly environment of space, and indeed this might be exactly how you would describe it in a log line. Be sure to make your antagonist clear. If your log line for "Raiders of the Lost Ark" was simply, "A swashbuckling archeologist searches for the Ark of the Covenant," we might picture two hours of our hero digging in the sand. Without the Nazis, there's no drama in that story.

Be careful not to let the goal of the antagonist overpower the goal of the protagonist. For example, you could describe the movie "Die Hard" as "a group of terrorists seize a building full of hostages as part of an elaborate heist. A lone cop must stop them." But this characterizes the protagonist (the cop) in a diminutive and reactive way. If instead we say, "a lone cop must overcome impossible odds to rescue his wife when he is trapped in a building seized by terrorists," you can see how the goal of the cop is emphasized. You'll notice that we made no mention of the leader of the antagonists in "Die Hard." The character of Hans Gruber (played by Alan Rickman) is one of the greatest bad guys in movie history, but he may not have a place in a log line for the film.

Sometimes the antagonist is also the protagonist of the story. This often happens when a story centers on a protagonist that must overcome some internal obstacle. In fact, many stories (and log lines) will have a component of personal obstacle that stands in the way of the protagonist's success. In "The Big Sick," the character of Kumail must overcome his *fear* of his parents' cultural disapproval if he wants to be with the woman he loves. This personal obstacle takes Kumail most of the film to overcome. (It would be inaccurate and weird if you described Kumail's *parents* as the antagonists.) In "Gravity," the protagonist is struggling with the death of a child, which affects her will to live in a survival situation. In "Breaking Bad," a dying chemistry teacher's desire to provide for his family by cooking meth collides with the allure of his new criminal lifestyle. But again, be careful. If your story is only about a character overcoming some personal defect, it can make your story sound very "internal" and uneventful. You might like the way "struggles with personal demons" sounds when describing your story about a boozy detective, but in a log line it will sound passive and boring.

The bottom line is this: good drama (and comedy) comes from the clear conflict of strong opposing forces. In addition to describing a protagonist with a strong need, make sure you succinctly describe the opposing force – or antagonist – in your log line.

The Set-Up. The last element of a log line is conveying a sense of the plot. We say "sense of plot" for two reasons. First, how much plot can you really capture in a sentence or two? Second, in most cases you will not really be describing the plot in a log line, but rather the thing that *incites* the bulk of the plot. The listener will then *infer* what happens in your plot. It might be more accurate to say you are describing the "scenario" or "set-up." In most log lines, this will be the element that conveys the concept. If it's a high-concept idea, we say the concept has a great "hook."

For example, in "Liar Liar" a lawyer must *tell the truth for an entire day*. Some readers might be thinking, "but isn't that the plot of the movie?" Yes and no. That is the set-up of the film, but does it tell you what happens in the film? With his family? With his court case? Not really. But the listener will understand that when a lawyer (someone who presumably lies for a living) has to tell the truth, mayhem will ensue, complicating the lawyer's entire world. In the best log lines, this element will be brief. And while you will never reveal your ending in a log line, ideally the desirable path to the ending should be clear. The listener will know what they *want* to see happen for the story to be resolved.

Ideally, all of the above elements should work together to accomplish this goal. Of course, every story presents a unique combination of challenges when it comes to crafting a great log line, based on all these elements. And an artful log line can take some liberty with the order of the elements. Just watch out for extraneous details.

* * *

Now that we've described our six guidelines for crafting a log line, we will take you through our process of creating one. We will build a stand-alone log line for the 1999 film "The Matrix" on the assumption that most of our readers will be familiar with it, and so will better understand the choices we make. Remember that we are building this log line as if it is our original story. This is very important because you have to take a step back and try to imagine explaining the film to someone who's never seen it. Some of the choices we make would also be helpful if we were crafting a longer version of this pitch.

Title/Rating/Genre

Our title is "The Matrix" – a pretty strong title, even if its meaning may not be clear in the log line. We think the finished film will be rated R, for action/violence and rough language. As for the genre, there are some decisions to make. The film has elements of fantasy, science fiction, action, and thrillers. As with many films, there is also a love story, but we think it would be a stretch to call it such. So, what to choose? As we've recommended, we'd like to limit the genre description to just two genres, if possible. While there are fantasy elements in the film, describing it as such would put it in the same category as "The Hobbit," and that's misleading. So, we will call it a "science fiction" film for its emphasis on machines and technology. But is that enough? What kind of science fiction is it? There are also elements of both action and thriller in the story, but if we picked just one, we would call it an "action" film because that better reflects what we think will be appealing about the idea. If we'd called it a "sci-fi thriller," that would better describe films like "Blade Runner" or "Inception."

Establish an unfamiliar setting

This is a little tricky. From the main character's point of view, the film is set in the present. So, nothing unfamiliar to establish. However, he will soon learn that the present is not what it seems to be and is, in fact, a rather complex illusion. This is a core aspect of the premise of the film so must be included in the log line even if it will not be fully explained until act two in the movie. This is an example of how we must consider the needs of the *log line* when it comes to explaining our story setting. If we merely described the setting as "a modern city," that would be both vague, and very misleading.

We will need to find a way to simplify and articulate what the Matrix *is* in a way that the listener will easily grasp and that captures the most critical aspects for understanding the story. Is the Matrix like a collective dream or hallucination? Maybe. But the problem with those two descriptions is that they imply something more medical in nature. Instead, we think describing the Matrix as a kind of "virtual reality" will be easier to understand because it sounds more technological and grounds something that is very complex in something that exists now. We'd never have time to explain the more elaborate, "technical" purpose of the Matrix (turning humans into batteries), nor how this unique world came to be (a war between humans and AI computers). And those aspects are not crucial to understanding the core premise of the story. But we might want to describe the Matrix's *intent* later on in the log line, when we identify the antagonist's goal.

Identify your protagonist

The main character is Thomas Anderson, also known as Neo. But proper nouns don't convey much information in a log line. It's better to describe the protagonist with both an adjective and a noun, and the ones we choose should be relevant to the story. So how do we identify the lead? Well, Anderson is a software engineer, but that's just his miserable day job and it doesn't really matter much to the plot of the film. More relevant, he's secretly known as Neo, a computer "hacker." It's *this* role that leads him to discover the Matrix – and that also brings the unwanted attention of the story's antagonist.

What adjective would be best to describe this hacker? We want to describe him in a way that both gives him personality and is also dramatically relevant. In other words, ask yourself, "Why *this* character in *this* story?" Ideally, it should be an adjective that casts our protagonist in a positive light, or at least not a negative one. So, what kind of hacker is he? What adjective would be dramatically relevant to this story? Well, we know the story is about Neo's difficult journey to becoming "The One" – a prophesized savior. Is Neo a "reluctant hacker"? Hmm, that makes him sound like he doesn't like to hack. Maybe a "cowardly hacker"? No, we think "cowardly" is too negative to be the description for a leading man, and it's not really accurate. Maybe "reclusive" works because it's Neo's withdrawn nature and lack of belief in himself that delays his rise to becoming "The One." We might have said "uninvolved," but again that also sounds a little too negative. "Reclusive" works.

Identify your protagonist's goal

Neo has several goals, as many movie heroes do. He must overcome his personal inhibitions (from reclusive to acceptance of his destiny) and become "The One." Some or all of this might make it into our log line. But Neo also wants to destroy the Matrix and free humanity from enslavement. This is the ultimate goal of the character, and it must be in the log line.

Identify the antagonist

Although Agent Smith is the key villain in the film, once again we are faced with the problem that proper nouns don't illuminate much. Even if you called him "the evil Agent Smith" we would be left to wonder who he is and what he's doing. So how do we characterize the antagonist? There might be some way to explain who he is, but it would likely be a lengthy description – not ideal when we are trying to do something in 50 words or less. So, let's just characterize the antagonist by saying it's the machines that enslave humanity. After all, Smith is just their representative in the story. To be sure, Smith would have a major role in a longer pitch, but he just may not be needed in a log line.

Notice that we introduced one more idea to the above: the goal of the antagonists – enslavement. This is important to note because it speaks to a fundamental narrative understanding you must have to craft a good log line, and a good pitch. If you don't understand that "The Matrix" is fundamentally, and dramatically, a story about a slave uprising, it will be hard to craft a good pitch for this story of any length. It's also why "Understanding Your Concept" gets an entire chapter of this book.

Set up the story

To set up the story in a log line you need to understand and identify the essential drama that occupies most of the film.

We could say that the drama involves defeating the machines, and that's okay, as far as it goes. However, remember that we only care about plot to the extent that it happens to someone we care about – the protagonist. So, what must Neo do to defeat the machines? He must become The One, right? This character transformation will take him 75% of the film, and this aspect is what you want to include in the log line when you set up the story.

Now let's put it all together and see what we've got.

"The Matrix" is an R-rated sci-fi, action film. A reclusive hacker discovers that the world is a virtual reality simulation, designed by AI machines to enslave humanity. To free mankind, he must become the savior prophesied to defeat them. (39 words)

Within this log line, you can see all the choices we laid out in our above analysis. If we wanted to expand this log line, we might have been able to introduce the idea of Morpheus and his team – the group that Neo joins to accomplish his goal. Or, we might have been able to imply what dramatic challenge the hacker will face to become the savior – but adding these things and keeping the log line under 50 words would have been a challenge.

If you're a beginner, this process probably looks a little daunting, but with practice it gets more instinctive and easier to do.

Again, this is a stand-alone log line. It's possible that a shorter, more oblique version might work for other purposes. For example:

A computer hacker discovers the world is an elaborate illusion, created by evil machines. (14 words)

Let's Create a Pitch

We're guessing that some readers who know the film will prefer this log line. However, it's so vague it wouldn't mean much to anyone unfamiliar with the story, and there's no drama. This type of log line would be of limited use – perhaps for a TV Guide listing. Or a similar version might be used as part of a longer pitch, where more information will soon be forthcoming. If you *didn't* know the film and all that you heard was this log line, the intent would be pretty nebulous.

Here are a few more examples of stand-alone log lines for some recent films you may have seen. If you know these films, look at the choices we made, based on the above 6 elements we described.

"The Avengers" is a PG-13 superhero film. A diverse team of superheroes is assembled by a secret government organization to defend Earth from an alien invasion. The superheroes must overcome their personal differences and work together to save the world. (41 words)

"Bad Moms" is a raunchy, R-rated comedy. Three overworked and underappreciated moms decide to go on a binge of fun, freedom, and self-indulgence. But the PTA leader and her clique of perfect moms are determined to get the rebels back in line. (42 words)

"Spy" is an R-rated action comedy about a dowdy but brilliant female CIA analyst must become a real spy when every other agent's cover is blown. She will have to find her inner James Bond if she's to stop an international arms dealer from launching a global disaster. (48 words)

"Wreck-it Ralph" is a PG animated comedy/adventure set inside the unseen world of video games. Ralph is a video game villain whose dream of becoming a hero accidentally threatens the game world. To save it, Ralph will have to become the hero he always wanted to be. (48 words)

"World War Z" is a PG-13 action/horror film. A UN employee must abandon his family to help stop a zombie apocalypse. Racing

against time, he travels the world to find the origin of the deadly pandemic that threatens to destroy humanity. (42 words)

"Arrival" is a PG-13 science fiction drama. When twelve mysterious extraterrestrial ships arrive on Earth, a lonely female linguist races to decipher the alien's strange language to prevent a global war. But as she begins to understand the aliens, she begins to understand the tragic loss she's suffered in life. (50 words)

(Note: If you've seen the movie "Arrival," you may notice that our log line is not technically accurate. But it reflects how the story is set up to avoid giving away the twist.)

"Baby Driver" is an R-rated crime thriller about a talented young getaway driver forced to help a gang of criminals. When a heist goes awry, the driver flees with his girlfriend, as both the gang and the police pursue him. (40 words)

"Get Out" is an R-rated horror movie. When a young black photographer accompanies his white girlfriend to her wealthy parents' estate, he discovers he is trapped in an evil, racist plot and must find a way to escape. (38 words)

What do you think? Do these examples capture the films you saw? Study these examples as much for what we left out as for what we included.

Now let's revisit the log line we proposed for our sample heist movie:

"'The Hostage' is an R-rated suspense/thriller. A loan officer befriends a quadriplegic customer only to discover his new friend is the mastermind behind an elaborate heist and revenge plot."

Does that fit the bill, based on the rules we just gave you? Let's see:

- Rating/Genre: As we said earlier, we intend it will be an R-rated Suspense/Thriller. Good.

- Protagonist: "A loan officer," established right up front, so we know whom we are following in the story. Very clear.
- Setting: Loan officers work in banks. A bank is a familiar place to most people, which shouldn't require any additional information – so all good.
- Describe the Protagonist: Hmm, we really don't know anything about the loan officer other than his job, so let's make another change. Let's call him a "helpful" loan officer. Why helpful? First, it makes the loan officer a more sympathetic character and second, it is the character's quality that the bad guy exploits, thus propelling the story.
- Antagonist: He's a quadriplegic who turns out to be a bank robber. Pretty good. This description doesn't overshadow the description of the good guy. Also, it's fresh: have you ever seen a film with a bad guy like this? And it might make the listener think, "How is that physically possible," and so implies the story will have surprises along the way. Intrigue is good.
- Set-Up: Here's what we have now, "only to discover his new friend is the mastermind behind an elaborate heist and revenge plot." Hmm, not great. Why? Because "discover" sounds too transient to make a great movie element. It suggests something like an "ah-ha" moment – and after *those* two seconds of screen time pass, then what happens? So let's change our log line one more time. What we want to do is better inform the listener of what will be happening for the bulk of the movie. How's this:

"'The Hostage' is an R-rated suspense/thriller. A helpful loan officer befriends a quadriplegic customer when the bank is robbed and everyone is taken hostage. As the loan officer tries to save himself and the hostages, he starts to suspect his quadriplegic friend is the mastermind behind the elaborate heist." (49 words)

As you can see, we replaced "discover" with "struggles to save," and added a little more intrigue by including "starts to suspect." Hopefully you see how both of these new phrases imply a greater sense of the movie's plot and also an unfolding mystery, as our hero uncovers the truth about his new "friend."

It is worth pointing out again that this stand-alone log line reveals twists (that the quadriplegic might be the mastermind) that a log line used in the context of a longer pitch might choose to hold back as a surprise. This plot twist is revealed here because in a situation where you are only going to deliver the log line, you will only get one shot to hook your listener. We have found that many beginners who pitch stand-alone log lines will sometimes hold back what's cool about their idea. The result is a pitch that under-sells itself. As screenwriter Paul Guay ("Liar Liar") likes to say, "When you pitch, don't make them hunt for the gold. That's your job!" And that is what we are trying to do here.

So what would our log line look like if it were *not* intended to be stand-alone but rather used in the context of a longer pitch? Maybe something like:

"A helpful loan officer befriends a quadriplegic customer when the bank is seized by a gang of robbers. The loan officer and his new friend must fight to save themselves and the other hostages."

Do you see how we establish all the elements of the drama but hold back our twist? As a stand-alone log line, it is less compelling, but remember, we will soon be elaborating on the story as we continue the pitch. In this longer version of the pitch, we will be able to build suspense and suspicion until we reveal that the quadriplegic is the criminal mastermind. Different pitches – different ambitions.

Log Lines: Comparing to Other Movies.

Comparing the project you are pitching to other films is one of the trickier things to pull off, and it takes some thought to do it right. The "it's X meets Y" pitch is a Hollywood cliché and can be more confusing than helpful. But if done right, comparing your project to similar movies can help establish the tone and other aspects of your story quickly and easily.

Here are a few tips to help guide you.

Use Contemporary Movies: If all of your comparisons or references are to 1940's movies, your idea will sound old-fashioned and possibly obscure. It will be obscure because, while many people in Hollywood are movie and television history buffs, some are not. Even for film buffs, an old film might be a vague memory. Or, they may only recall some unfavorable aspect of your choice of comparison. For example, making reference to a well-known film like Frank Capra's 1946 film "It's a Wonderful Life" is full of risks. While few will challenge the film's stature in film history, many recall the film to be emblematic of a soft and corny tone, hence the phrase "Capra-corn." (Not to mention the film famously flopped when it was released.) It's better to compare your film to ones that were released within the past five years. Even if you are pitching a remake of a vintage film, this is a wise thing to do. After all, you are most likely there to explain to the listener how you plan to update the vintage film.

Use Successful Movies: Comparing your movie to monumental flops is not a good way to sell anything. Hollywood values success over all other values. Use well-known and successful Hollywood movies. This will increase the chance that others will be familiar with the reference in a positive way. If your listeners haven't heard of the Hungarian art house film you use as an example, it does you no good at all.

There are some caveats to this advice. There are different kinds of perceived successes in Hollywood, and we are not saying you should only make comparisons to films that grossed, say, $100 million at the box office. There are some films that may have only grossed a moderate amount but are considered triumphs in their own right. "Happy Death Day" is a good example. The film got mixed reviews but grossed $56 million in the U.S. and only cost $5 million to produce, so it is regarded as a very viable horror/comedy, relative to its cost. On the flip side of this calculation, a film like "Life of Pi" grossed almost $120 million in the U.S. but might be considered too artistic or idiosyncratic to a single filmmaker to make it a good comparison. There are some movies that executives believe can only succeed when done by a certain writer or director. Finding the best film comparison is not just about box office, though. Pitching your film by comparing it to top-grossing films like "Titanic" or "Avatar" can seem like a crass over-reach. On the artistic end of the spectrum, the day after "The Artist" won the Academy Award for Best Picture, not one studio was seeking to emulate the film, despite its virtues.

Make Your Comparison Clear: Too often inexperienced writers toss off comparisons to other films where their intent is unclear. "It's like 'The Avengers' meets 'Taken.'" What does that mean? Maybe the meaning will be clear in the context of your pitch, but maybe not. It might be better to say, "It's about a team of heroes who have to work together, like in 'The Avengers,' but with a grittier tone, like 'Taken.'" In this latter example, it is more specific and clear what exactly you are trying to pull out of your comparison.

If you are still unsure about making comparisons, it is probably best *not* to do it. Or, if you are pitching your project with a producer, allow her or him to set the stage for the pitch, including film comparisons, prior to launching into your pitch.

So what is the real value of making comparisons?

The upsides are the positive associations and improved clarity they can create in the mind of your listener. It should be self-evident why a convincing comparison to a hit film might be beneficial. This is Hollywood, after all. Understanding the value of clarity in areas of tone and genre cannot be over-estimated. The challenge of pitching, and even writing, is the challenge of conveying an artistic "vision" from one person to another. This is a difficult thing to do, and the people who do it are always trying to find a common artistic vocabulary to make the job easier. Comparisons can be valuable tools in this effort. They help the listener imagine how the story you describe will be realized. If you were pitching our bank heist story, your listener is going to picture it very differently if you compare it to "Ocean's Eleven" than if you compare it to "The Town."

Imagine you were pitching something like "Austin Powers: International Man of Mystery." If you launched right into the plot without establishing the tone, would the listener know it was a parody? Or would they think you were a really bad writer pitching a really bad sci-fi/spy movie?

"The Bourne Identity" and its sequels are in the same genre and have the same rating as the older James Bond movies, but James Bond has a more fantastical, light-hearted tone while Bourne films are more gritty and realistic. A villain with steel teeth named "Jaws" fits into Bond's world but not into Bourne's. (Ironically, after the success of the Bourne movies, the James Bond franchise became more gritty and realistic.)

Using comparisons can head off a buyer's concerns before they occur. If there's something about your idea that feels difficult or non-commercial, finding some recent, successful films that had the same element can ease the buyer's mind. For example, if your story is about a character that is alone for a large amount of time, you might compare it to "Castaway." However, be sure that the comparisons are really similar or it will just highlight the problem. In "Castaway," there was an inanimate character (the Wilson volleyball) for the main character to interact with. If your story doesn't have a similar device, you haven't really eased the buyer's mind.

Even if you choose not to make use of comparisons to other films as part of your pitch – and it is perfectly fine not to – you should still be prepared to make them because the buyer might very well ask you what other films are like yours. Being able to reference two or three recent, successful films when needed will go a long way to putting the buyer at ease as to the viability of your idea.

Introducing the World and Rules.

Once you've given a good log line and your listener knows your concept, you are able to spend some time setting up your story by describing things like the setting and characters. The log line allows the listener to understand the significance of these elements. It gives everything to come some context. At this stage, most writers will launch into a description of the world in which their story takes place. (If it's an original story – if it's a rewrite, adaptation or director pitch, the setting might already be clear.) Depending on your subject matter it may already be clear. If your one-liner is comparable to our sample bank heist film, the setting may be super-clear: a bank. Nevertheless, there are many stories that require more time and effort than, "Fade in. It was a typical day at the bank…"

Some genres, like science fiction and fantasy, take place in an unfamiliar world that has to be established before you can delve into your story. This can be particularly challenging in a pitch. If it takes you ten minutes to describe the setting of your story, you risk boring the listener and using up time needed for character and story. You have to think carefully about how to set up the world efficiently. What aspects of the world are critical to the story? In "Children of Men," the fact that humans have lost the ability to reproduce is critical, as is the fact that Britain has walled itself off from the outside world. However, the slightly futuristic advances in computers or cars are irrelevant and could be skipped in that pitch. When pitching science fiction, you should give a time frame – is this ten years in the future? A hundred? Thousands? This can help you establish much of the context and you'll only need to highlight the most relevant technologies. Fantasy is harder, but if you can compare it to something we know – medieval Europe, for example – you might be able to shorthand it for the listener.

This challenge can also occur in stories that are not science fiction or fantasy. A pitch with a historical setting may require some context for the politics or customs of the era. Would you be able to pitch the hit series "Downton Abbey" without first establishing the highly specific cultural aspects of England in the early 20th century? Even a realistic, contemporary story can have a specialized world that requires some description. If you were pitching a movie like "The Big Sick," you might need to describe the culture of Pakistani immigrants living in the U.S.

The other thing you'll need to do is establish the rules of any magic, supernatural elements, or speculative technology. If you fail to clearly delineate what can and can't be done in the world you're attempting to portray, you risk confusing your listener or looking like you are making things up as you go along. For example, Harry Potter can perform numerous magical feats, but the filmmakers establish that this is what a wizard does and that they need a special wand to do it. Rules. Sometimes, if there's only one unusual thing or rule in your story, it can be revealed in the course of the story. For example, in the science fiction/horror film "The Fly," you could describe the rules of the teleportation devices when you explain how the hero invented them. However, if your world depends on these elements, you may need to address them up front. This applies not just to science fiction and fantasy, but also to supernatural horror, superhero movies, and other stories with these elements. Set up only the rules that will become dramatically necessary or relevant in your story. Be specific and clear.

Fortunately, our heist movie doesn't require the establishment of a specialized world. However, it's possible some of the plot twists could depend on the listener understanding the way bank security works or the unique physical or medical challenges of a person who is paralyzed. In the case of our sample story, it should be possible to add this information as it comes up in the body of the pitch. Indeed, conveying this information up front in our pitch might tip our hand and ruin a surprise in the story. And it may even be better for the listener to learn this information at the same time as the lead character. This is typical of the reasoning you must apply when deciding how to handle unique worlds or special rules in the world you are portraying.

Introducing Main Characters.

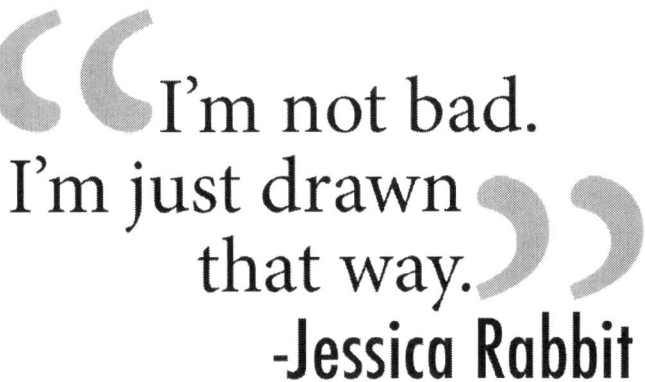

> "I'm not bad.
> I'm just drawn
> that way."
> -Jessica Rabbit

Once you've successfully introduced the nature of your project, it's time to dive into the actual story you want to tell. We've been calling this "the plot" of your story even though we've advised you that it's really more than this.

First, you will need a strategy to introduce your main characters. You will have to decide whether to present your characters as they appear in the normal course of your story or introduce them before you launch into your plot.

You may want to set up your characters before the plot if establishing your main character requires a long description. In this situation, you might not want to stop the flow of your story for a long-winded aside. Perhaps your listener needs to understand the past or "back story" of a character to make a plot point in the story work. In the script, you might handle this by using a flashback or a short preamble, but both of these devices can be deadly in a pitch unless the events they present are very dramatic. If you are pitching "Thor," you will need some time to explain who he is!

In our heist story, it shouldn't be difficult to establish John's character as we meet him. In the first few scenes we can easily dramatize what John does for a living, how he tries to help customers (including Tony, the quadriplegic customer) and how this causes conflict with his boss, Kent.

On the other hand, what if a significant plot point of our heist story required the listener to understand something that happened to John in his childhood? We may not want to have a flashback in the pitch, or describe the scene where John tells Tony this information in the course of their growing friendship. If the story about John's childhood is really important, we might want to tell the listener about John's character, including this incident, before we launch into plot.

Another reason to establish your character up front is if you have multiple lead characters in your film, and you're afraid that introducing too many characters in the body of your pitch will confuse the listener. This situation can occur if you are pitching an "ensemble piece." (A story that features multiple major characters sharing screen time.)

Frequently it is better to start off by describing each member of the ensemble in comparison to each other, focusing on the key similarities and differences that are critical to the thematic elements of the story. So, if you were pitching "Girls Trip," you might want to describe the four old friends that compose the "flossy posse." Or, if you were pitching "Little Miss Sunshine," you might start by describing the six members of the family.

It can be easier for the listener if essential characters are not referred to by their names but rather by what they *do* or how they are *related* to the main character. Using our heist example again, John's branch manager's name is Kent, but as we pitch it may be clearer if we just refer to him as "John's boss," after his initial introduction. Once you've given more than about three or four names, it will be difficult for the listener to remember who's who. Don't let this happen. As we've said, your characters are your listener's way into your story. If they forget who is *who* along the way, that's bad.

Another aspect of introducing characters has to do with how you describe them in ways that allow your listener to understand their essential nature quickly and efficiently. There's a little bit of poetry involved in this challenge, especially if you decide to introduce your characters in the body of your pitch where brevity is key. Naturally, some of your character descriptions will involve things like their job, their age, or their sex. The more difficult task is helping your listener get a grasp on your character's personality in a concise but vivid way. One trick is to identify two significant traits for your main character: one strength, and one weakness. In our heist example, we might describe John as, "A 20-something loan officer. The kind of guy who will give you the shirt off his back, then buy it back from you at a mark-up." We could have just said John is "generous but gullible," but we hope you see that this latter version lacks the same poetry. What you are establishing in the pitch are the key characteristics, desires and flaws that will come into play in the story. You will likely reveal far more about the character in the script, and know even more than that before you start writing. Again, the goal here is the best fifteen-minute version of the story.

Main Characters: Casting Suggestions.

When you pitch, it is not unusual that your listener might ask what actors you have in mind for the leading roles. (Or you might reference casting suggestions without being asked.) As with referencing other films, you should always have an answer ready to this question, but doing so is just as tricky as what films you reference. Here are a few tips for doing it right.

- Unlike referencing a specific film, most talented actors will have played a variety of roles. So by referencing an actor for your lead, you are really referencing a specific character the actor played in one of their films. There's nothing wrong with this as long as what you mean is clear.
- Don't limit your casting choices. If you imply there are only a few actors in the world that could possibly play the characters you are pitching, you are shooting yourself in the

foot. Cast-ability is one of the important things buyers will be considering as they listen to your pitch, and it might partly determine whether or not they will buy it. The more actors who can play the roles, the more likely the project will get made. This is especially true when it comes to the ages of your characters. Allow a range. Sometimes a character must be a specific age for the story to work, but otherwise say things like "mid-20's" or "in her 30's" or "around 40." The exception is if your characters are children where a difference of a couple years is huge. In those cases, give exact ages.

- If the main characters in the story you are pitching are under the age of 18, you are all but guaranteeing that project must be cast with unknowns, or at least not well-established actors. This is not a deal breaker, but if the budget required to make your final product is huge, it might be a factor in the buyer's decision-making process. (Sometimes, Hollywood prefers to cast well-known actors to "hedge their bet" on a higher-budget production.) If this is what you are pitching, do your best to find the biggest names that are right for the roles and be prepared to justify why they might have a following.
- Buyers tend not to develop pitches that feature main characters in their 60s, 70s, and 80s. Yes, we all love Tommy Lee Jones, Meryl Streep, Harrison Ford, Al Pacino, and Robert De Niro. And while we encourage you to follow your passion, if it means writing scripts for these brilliant actors, just be aware that not many of these projects are sold from pitches unless these stars are attached to the pitch.
- Be sure to pick actors that are both well-known and well respected. The names you reference need to be famous enough so that the listener won't need to check The Internet Movie Database (IMDb.com) to figure out whom you're suggesting. Also, if you are using an actor as reference to describe your main character, it will certainly help the project feel commercial if the example you give is a big star. By and large, there is almost no upside to referencing an actor who isn't a big star for your lead character. Additionally, although the list of big stars is ever changing, picking the wrong one can mislead the buyer about your intentions. Ultimately,

buyers may be willing to make your script with a fine actor like Viggo Mortensen, but they will be more likely to develop your script if you suggest it's intended for Chris Pratt. To do it right, you must be current with Hollywood culture and the ever-shifting ebb and flow of stardom. If you are a writer pitching with a producer or director, it's sometimes better to leave the casting suggestions to him or her. If you are a producer or director, casting is an important part of your pitch.

We will continue our discussion of character in the context of the plot, where these issues might become a little clearer.

Plot.

> " A story should have a beginning, a middle and an end, but not necessarily in that order. "
> -Jean-Luc Godard

If you're doing a full-length pitch of an original story (or any pitch longer than 2 or 3 minutes), we urge you to pitch your plot by articulating act breaks. Three acts are the custom when pitching motion pictures, while television uses anywhere from two to seven acts, depending on format. While not every script or finished film has clear act breaks, the use of act breaks when pitching is essential. In ad-sponsored television, the use of act breaks is even more entrenched because they define the commercial breaks. It is the tradition in television to not only pitch act breaks but also sometimes to indicate them in the final written teleplay. (Although when pitching a series, you may not pitch an episode story at all. We will discuss this in more detail in the chapter on pitching television). In feature films, act breaks are based more on dramatic theory, but because three acts are the way the industry talks about structure, you should be familiar with the theory.

There are two main reasons to articulate act breaks in your pitch. One, act breaks help convey a sense of the timeline of your final product. If your listener has to ask where you are in your story (from a screen-time perspective), you're in trouble. Two, act breaks help you frame and "punctuate" the significant story beats as you pitch: set-up, complication and resolution.

Describing act structure and how to use it in writing is beyond the scope of this book. For more information about how to use act structure, we suggest you read "The Three Stages of Screenwriting" by Douglas Eboch. But for the purposes of pitching motion pictures, the key elements are:

Act One takes up about the first fourth of the movie. It sets up the world, the main characters, their dilemmas and the stakes.

Act Two is the middle half of the movie and is where the character faces obstacles to achieving their goal while changing as a person.

Act Three is roughly the final quarter of the movie and contains the dramatic and climactic resolution to the story. Significant character issues and conflicts are also resolved.

Act structure in scripted, ad-supported television depends on the format. The predominant formats and their respective act structures usually break down as:

1-Hour Drama: A teaser, followed by four or five acts.

Half-hour Comedy: A cold open, followed by two acts, and sometimes a tag at the end.

Two-Hour Television Movie: Pitched in 3 or 7 acts for ad-supported television, and pitched in 3 acts (like a feature film) for non-ad-supported television. If your listener has questions at the end of your pitch, they will refer back to these general areas using this same terminology.

Be aware that act break structure for 1-hour drama and half-hour comedy varies by series and whether or not the series is intended for commercial or non-commercial television.

One caveat – when you pitch, you don't want to sound like you followed a formula. Overdoing screenwriting terminology during the pitch can make it sound like you just finished some screenwriting book last weekend. The buyer wants to hear a story that you're passionate about, and not one that feels manufactured. So the act breaks should only be signposts, not the focus of your pitch. Don't forget, you're telling a story, not building a bridge.

In order to best convey the experience of your movie in a 15-minute verbal form, you're going to have to let go of some of the plot details and focus on the major story sequences (sometimes called "arcs"). These sequences convey the broad strokes of character and story as they unfold over the course of the pitch.

In motion pictures, Act One takes up more time in a pitch because you have to establish the characters, their world, their goals and flaws, as well as the hook that launches the story. This is where the use of act breaks can really help. Without using act breaks your listener may think your first act takes up as much as half your story because of the disproportionate time the set-up can take to pitch.

Despite the extra time that the set-up takes, don't skip through this stuff too quickly or you risk the listener becoming confused. Probably the most important thing – and most commonly overlooked – is taking the time to set up the main character (and possibly some of the supporting characters), and *why* we will care about them. It's a mistake to assume your listener will have a natural affinity with your protagonist unless you clearly create one. Beginners struggle with this aspect of pitching because they will assume that the listener will inherently love their protagonists. But this is not so, and you must provide an active reason. This is especially critical to do with so-called "anti-hero" main characters. If you don't interest the listener in the main character, there is no reason for them to care about the outcome of the story – just like in the movie.

Also, in a pitch, it is tough to rely on the natural course of your story (as it would be presented in a screenplay) to adequately establish and explain the things that define your main characters. Unlike in a screenplay, where the main character's virtues might be revealed dramatically over the course of the entire story, you don't have this same luxury in a pitch. You want your listener to grasp your character's virtues as soon as possible. Even in a story with an irascible character, like Clint Eastwood's character in "Gran Torino," you'll want to give the listener a reason to care. In such a case, you might describe Eastwood's Walt Kowalski character as "crusty but honest to a fault, always willing to do the right thing, even when doing so is dangerous."

Let's use our bank heist example again. In that story, it takes some time for our main character – loan officer John – to rise to the challenges he faces in the story, confronting the bank robbers in the third act and foiling their plan. Unless our pitch specifically articulates the virtues of John's character up front, we will spend most of the pitch with a main character that will seem passive. So, we might want to say, "We meet our main character John, who is the most decent loan officer you'll ever meet, always on the verge of being fired for his compassionate treatment of his customers." Right up front we know why John deserves our attention – he is an exceptionally caring person, actively putting the needs of others before his own. This set-up also has the added benefit of explaining why bad guy Tony is able to pray upon John's good nature early in the story, and also why John puts himself on the line to save the bank's customers.

By the conclusion of Act One, you should clearly establish the primary conflict your character(s) will grapple with for the bulk of the story, and you should do so in a way that is cinematic. In the case of our heist story, a natural act break might be the Head Bank Robber yelling, "Nobody move, this is a robbery!" Even better and more cinematic, we could conclude Act One with the flashing lights and screeching tires of the police and S.W.A.T team arriving on the scene. You can also combine this with some character aspect. Perhaps loan officer John would have been safely out of the bank and on his lunch break when the robbery occurs had he not decided to stay and help quadriplegic Tony finish his loan application. No good deed goes unpunished – we can all relate to that.

After you describe the Act One turning point, you can talk more generally about the tensions and arcs that drive the story through Act Two. Remember, you only have a few minutes to describe a second act that will take place over the course of an hour or so on screen. This can be a tricky thing to accomplish in a pitch. You will need to describe any major twists in the plot, but you want to be careful not to fall into the monotony of, "this happens, then this happens, then this happens…" In our heist example, we think the most important events in Act Two include: John learning how Tony became quadriplegic, their decision to escape, Tony volunteering to be a decoy, John leading the other hostages to safety, John discovering explosives planted by the robbers, and John rescuing Tony. Act Two concludes with John learning that Tony has conned him and is, in fact, the mastermind of the heist. Notice how all of the plot points we listed involve the direct actions of the protagonist. That's not an accident. As we've said, the minute you lose focus on the character is the minute your pitch will become uninvolving.

Just as important as what we included in Act Two is what we left out of it. For example, there may be a scene where John helps Tony fix something that breaks on his wheelchair, but since that isn't a major plot twist, we might leave it out, depending on the length of the pitch.

In addition to citing the major plot points, it will also help to describe an overview of the way things change throughout Act Two. When pitching our heist movie, we might say something like, "Throughout the beginning of the ordeal, John and Tony are becoming friends." In the script, we'll need to craft scenes to show this, but in a pitch, it is necessary to summarize. The shorter the pitch, the more summarizing you'll need to do.

Again, make sure that you are not just focusing on the actions or the mechanics of plotting. You must stay relentlessly focused on how the main character(s) experiences these events. We've seen many writers who are able to successfully establish character and set-up in their first act but then fail to continue developing the character as the story progresses. You need to track the character's arc and the changing relationships between the characters with as much attention as you track the physical plot events. This can be expressed generically as, "What does the character want, what do they learn, how do they react, what do they do?"

In our heist example, John wants to survive and help others to survive. The plot is the robbery. But John learns the heist is not as it appears to be, and he may have even helped facilitate the heist because Tony duped him. How John reacts to and overcomes these evolving circumstances should play a significant part of Act Two. John will have to change and grow as a person. The mild-mannered loan officer will have to summon up a depth of courage he didn't know he had. Again, "What does John want, what does John learn, how does John react, what does John do?"

Plot: The Ending.

If your story is properly structured, the end of act two should spin it off in a new direction for act three. In the case of our heist movie, at the end of the second act John loses his biggest ally and the story moves from suspense to action. John will be on his own and will have to grow as a character to succeed. You will need to go into a little more detail at the climax, trying to make it as dramatic and exciting as possible so that you end your pitch with a bang. But don't forget the character. You want to be clear about how the story has changed the character and affected their life.

The ending of our heist movie will include a chase and fight, but we must also describe how this sequence allows John to overcome his overly cautious nature to do what must be done to save the innocent victims. You should always end your pitch on a dramatic and conclusive note. Occasionally, writers will get to the end of the pitch and just kind of trail off before saying, "Yeah…that's it." This is as unsatisfying as watching a movie and learning it's over only because the theater lights came on. The way your story ends is crucial. It is the last thing your listener will remember about your story. Think about the feeling you want the audience to experience in those final moments. Our heist story will end with John having grown as a character and thwarted the heist. He's still a good guy, but to dramatize his new self-awareness, his last act in the film will be to emphatically stamp bad-guy Tony's loan application as "rejected"! Very satisfying. You want your pitch to have an ending that is conclusive and that clearly resolves the primary dramatic conflicts in the story. But you also want an ending that "punctuates" that moment for your listener.

In any pitch longer than five minutes, you should always resolve the story. Remember, the purpose of a pitch that length is more than just a teaser. We are amazed when we hear people give the opposite advice: "Never give away your ending." Don't listen to them. You're asking the buyer to pay you a lot of money for your story. They're not going to do that if they don't know that you have a good ending. This does not necessarily apply to shorter pitches where, say, you're trying to get someone to read an existing script. In this scenario, you probably don't want to give everything away. Your goal is to give the potential reader just enough so they will want to read the script, where they know an ending exists. However, if they ask for the ending, you should be prepared to tell them what it is.

Similarly, don't give choices. Sometimes new writers will offer two possible endings or other plotting choices to the listener. The writer's thought is they could do either way and want to pick the one the buyer likes best. But buyers don't want to do your work for you. They don't want to choose. They want you to tell a good story with the best ending you can create. So take a point of view. Don't be afraid of bold choices, if you can justify them.

Plot: Using Set Pieces.

Now that you've mapped out the major plot points and character arcs, let's back up for a moment. During a full-length pitch, you'll want to identify the major "set pieces" in your story. The exact definition of a set piece is a little fuzzy, but typically it means an elaborately constructed and memorable scene or sequence of scenes in a film. In an action movie, the set pieces will usually be the big action scenes. In a comedy, the outrageously funny scenes. In a drama the gut wrenching, emotional scenes. In a horror movie the shocking and scary scenes. Notice we used the word "memorable" when describing what a set piece is. Buyers like set pieces because, in addition to being an enjoyable part of the story, set pieces are frequently the thing the audience will talk about when recommending the film to others. Positive "word-of-mouth" (as it is referred to in distribution circles) is probably the most important thing that drives box office success after the opening weekend of a film, even more important than good reviews or advertising.

Most experienced writers will integrate their set pieces into the flow of their pitch and, as they appear, will identify them as such to the listener. If you don't integrate your set pieces into your pitch, be prepared to identify them if the buyer asks about them at the conclusion of your pitch. When you pitch your set pieces, avoid pitching them as scenes. Instead, describe in general what makes the set piece interesting, compelling or memorable. So for example, if you were pitching the final attack on the Death Star at the end of the original "Star Wars" as a set piece, you'd want to describe it as more than just an "epic battle," or a series of laser blasts and explosions. You'd want to explain how dramatic it will be to see Luke Skywalker, in his tiny X-Wing Fighter, repeatedly try and fail to navigate the canals of the massive Death Star, and it's only when Luke learns to trust the force that he's able to take that "one-in-a-million" shot, destroying the Death Star. This description incorporates action, but also drama and character. Much better.

Plot: Using dialog.

While dialog is pervasive in a script, it is used far more sparingly in most pitches, and almost never in a pitch that is five minutes or shorter. There is no law against you articulating a character's dialog in a pitch of any length, and in some cases it can be helpful. Unfortunately, many writers include dialog in a pitch only because they love the sound of their own voice. If you're going to include dialog in your pitch, let's consider a few ways it can be helpful.

Brevity: Brevity is always a priority when trying to condense a two-hour film down to fifteen minutes. Sometimes the judicious use of a character's dialog can be great shorthand for something it would take much longer to describe. This could be a plot twist or some other story revelation. For example, if you were pitching "Casablanca," you might say, "Ilsa turns to Rick and says, 'You see, Victor Laszlo is my husband... and was even when I knew you in Paris.'" Imagine instead if you just describe the events. It might go something like this: "It's at that moment in the story when Ilsa turns to Rick and reveals that, not only is she currently married to Victor Laszlo, but that she was also married to Victor when she and Rick were having an affair in Paris." The latter version is more elaborate and has less impact.

Characterization: A good line of dialog can help your listener zero-in on the "voice" or attitude or some other quality of characterization that would be tough to convey just through description. From "Casablanca," Rick's line, "I stick my neck out for nobody" is a good example. We also could have said, "Rick's the kind of guy who doesn't like to get involved with other people's problems." Accurate, but not very colorful.

Tone: Conveying tone is one of the best uses of dialog in a pitch. As we've discussed, tone is one of the hardest things to express when pitching. The occasional use of dialog can help let your listener identify what you intend. Is it a witty adult drama or is it an R-rated teen comedy? This is particularly true in comedy. In order to make your pitch funny, you'll need to include some jokes, and those are often expressed through dialog. If you were pitching the restaurant scene from "When Harry Met Sally...," you might say: "Sally fakes an orgasm to prove Harry can't tell a fake from the real thing. Sally is so convincing that another customer turns to her waiter and says, 'I'll have what she's having.'" Telling a joke this way will make your pitch funny. But you should select your jokes carefully. When we picked this line of dialogue from "When Harry Met Sally..." it was no coincidence it is one of the most memorable moments in the film. While it perfectly represents the feisty nature of the relationship (and conflict) between Harry and Sally, it plays no role in the plot.

As we said previously, there may be occasions where a writer will add details to their pitch that they know will not end up in the final product. Don't be afraid to add these details to your pitch if you believe that adding them will help capture the spirit and intentions of your story. There's nothing wrong with doing so, and buyers understand that this can happen.

For example, you might use a great comedic one-liner that helps sell the tone of a scene, or you might want to describe your main character in a way that you feel captures their "essence." Describing Rick in "Casablanca" as a "guy that sticks his neck out for nobody" might capture his essence, even if that line never appeared in the script. Same thing with our heist film and this is why we described the lead as the kind of guy who would "give you the shirt off his back, and then buy it back from you at a mark-up."

Of course, turning in a script to the buyer that deviates *significantly* from the pitch that sold the story is considered unprofessional, or worse.

While most pitches can be told along the lines we just presented, there are many stories that will require special accommodations. As we've said, some science fiction and fantasy stories will require more of your time and efforts establishing the unique features of the world you're presenting. Stories that use magic will require careful explanation of the rules. Thrillers and mysteries are usually tougher to pitch because they are often plot heavy, so you'll need to pay special attention to simplifying and clarifying the most important plot points. Ensemble pieces will require more time spent on character description and making sure each character is distinct. Also, the genre of your project influences your emphasis: An action movie will emphasize "set pieces" more, while a romantic comedy will focus on the character's emotional growth. All that your listener will know is what you tell them, so you must be sure you are giving them all the information they need to understand your story.

What about Shorter Pitches?

We've given you an outline of the elements of a pitch that lasts ten to fifteen minutes, but as we pointed out in the introduction to this book, some situations (in fact, *most* situations) call for shorter pitches.

So how do you reduce? First, remember what is most important: hook and character. To shrink your pitch, you should condense your plot first. As we've mentioned, most shorter pitches (less than 5-minutes) will *not* attempt to take the listener through the entire story. Second, identify and summarize the arcs of the story rather than the events. The shorter the pitch, the more important it is to be clear about who the main characters are and how your story will change them. For example, a 2-minute pitch will likely have similar intentions as a 2-minute trailer. It will emphasize concept, main characters, hook and a little bit of "sizzle" (what is fun or provocative about your topic). At this length, your pitch will consist mostly of set-up and probably not give away the ending (as with a trailer). Once your pitch has been compressed down to 15 or 30 seconds, all you'll really be pitching is the concept in the form of a log line – the hook and the character.

With our heist concept, it's possible a 30-second pitch may give away a significant twist or two. If all you have is 30 seconds to sell your pitch and you think those twists are essential to what's great about the idea, don't hold back. If you're pitching "The Sixth Sense" in 30 seconds you may not want to give away that big surprise ending, but it might not be a bad idea to indicate there *is* a big surprise ending.

It's rare that a writer will do a pitch of less than five minutes with the goal of immediately being hired to write a screenplay or teleplay. Usually, these pitches will be used to interest the buyer in hearing a longer pitch at a later date, or in reading a completed screenplay. So you do not have to give them everything – you need to give them the most interesting elements of your story. Always construct the best version of the story for the length you are presenting.

Now that we've spent the last eighty-five pages or so laying out all the complexities of pitching, let's create an actual pitch so you can see how it's really done.

"Gravity": 2-Minute Pitch.

We will start with a sample 2-minute pitch for the film "Gravity." We chose "Gravity" because it is recent, critically acclaimed, and very successful, so we think there's a good chance most of you will have seen it. Unlike our heist example, this will allow you to read an actual pitch where you know the story. That way you can see what aspects of the film we included and omitted from our 2-minute pitch. In fact, we will give you *two* versions so you can see how pitching approaches can vary while still following the plan that we've laid out.

Remember, a 2-minute pitch is not intended to result in a sale, but rather could be used to get someone interested in reading your spec script or hearing a longer version of your pitch. For these two versions of "Gravity," we will leave in the section headings for the sake of clarity, but of course they would never be part of an actual pitch.

"Gravity" – Version One

Personal Connection

Most people are amazed when I tell them that there have been 135 space shuttle missions. An astronaut working in space is a miracle that's become so commonplace we take it for granted. We forget that space travel is the most dangerous job in the world – even if you're orbiting 350 miles above it. This is a movie that reminds us that it can all go wrong – horribly wrong, in an instant – and I call it….

Title

… "Gravity"!

Genre/Rating/Tone

"Gravity" is a contemporary PG-13, survival/thriller and here's the idea…

Log Line

Two Astronauts face a life or death struggle when space debris utterly annihilates their shuttle, leaving them stranded – floating in space. With no hope of rescue, the Astronauts must work together to find a way to survive.

Characters

The story focuses almost exclusively on our two leads – Mission Specialist Dr. Ryan Stone on her first shuttle mission and veteran

Astronaut Matt Kowalski. She's a career scientist, struggling with the recent loss of her child. He's a classic, levelheaded, leading man with all the right stuff. She is as green as he is self-confident.

Story (set-up)

The story opens with Ryan and Matt space-walking, repairing the Hubble when they get an emergency call from Mission Control – a nearby satellite has exploded and a field of space debris is headed their way – at 18,000 MPH! But they learn too late and the debris field hits their shuttle, destroying it and killing the rest of their crew.

At the end of act one, panicked Ryan and seasoned Matt are stranded, floating in space, with no way home, and nothing keeping them alive but the oxygen in their suits!

Together in the hostile nothingness of space, and with the deadly debris retuning in 90 minutes, Matt and Ryan have to think fast.

Working together and against the clock, Matt and Ryan devise a desperate but ingenious plan to use abandoned space stations from the past 20 years as a way to survive and get back home. With no hope of rescue and no contact with Mission Control, all they will have is each other.

"Gravity" – Version Two

Personal Connection

Did you know that survival experts say the single biggest factor determining whether someone survives a life-threatening situation, such as getting lost in the wilderness, is whether or not they <u>believe</u> they can survive? Those that believe set about figuring out how to do it, while the others give up. And probably the most dangerous place human beings venture today is into the vacuum of outer space. So I want to tell a story about astronauts trying to survive a disaster in orbit. I call it...

Title

... *"Gravity"!*

Genre/Rating/Tone

"Gravity" is a realistic, contemporary PG-13, survival/thriller...

Log Line

...about two astronauts, a rookie and a veteran, who have to figure out how to get back to Earth after their shuttle is destroyed by debris.

Characters

Mission Specialist Ryan Stone is a career scientist, struggling to overcome the recent death of her daughter. Dr. Stone's work has landed her on the space shuttle for her first mission. Veteran Astronaut Matt Kowalski is on his final mission. Ryan never wanted to be an astronaut. Space makes her anxious – Matt loves it.

Story (set-up)

We open with Ryan and Matt space-walking so Ryan can upgrade the Hubble telescope. Suddenly, an emergency call comes in from Mission Control – a satellite has exploded and a field of debris is headed their way – at 18,000 MPH! But the warning comes too late. The debris hits their shuttle, destroying it and killing the rest of their crew. Communication has been lost. Ryan and Matt are stranded, quickly running out of air, with nobody to rely on but each other. Ryan is panicked. Matt, the level-headed pro, calms her.

Working against the clock, Matt devises a desperate but ingenious plan to travel miles through the void to the abandoned international space station where there is air – and if they're lucky, an escape pod.

But when the plan goes awry, Ryan will have to overcome her fear and doubt and decide that she has what it takes to survive. Only then will she be able to muster the will to attempt a risky reentry in a damaged capsule... with nobody to rely on but herself.

See how much variation can be achieved while still following the guidelines we've laid out? Compare the two versions. Think about the choices we made in each, and what you might have done differently.

Pay special attention to the different personal connections we used and why we chose them. You might notice that neither of them is specifically "personal." But each offers a unique "personal insight" that helps establish something useful for the pitch that follows.

"Die Hard": 5-Minute Pitch.

Next, let's try a longer pitch. What follows is a 5-minute pitch of another great film we've referenced in this book, "Die Hard." We will leave out the section headings this time so you can read our version without interruption. You will notice there are two major differences between this pitch and the 2-minute pitches we did for "Gravity." 1) We will go into a lot more detail in the plot section of the pitch and 2) rather than "teasing" the story, the 5-minute version will summarize the entire story.

Although a 5-miute pitch is not a full-length pitch, we think it will be helpful for you to see how we approach the level of detail it requires. Other than running time, there's not really that much difference between constructing a 5-minute pitch and a full 10 or 15-minute pitch. Both lengths require a presentation of plot that is complete, with a beginning, middle and end. A longer version would simply require more detail. If you can do one well, you can do the other.

Still, this pitch will omit many plot details, as *you* will have to do, if you try to distill a 131-minute film into five minutes.

As you read through the story summary, notice how we try to keep the pitch focused on the hero – John McClane – and how he experiences the story. Also notice that we keep the tone dramatic but give the listener signposts in the form of act breaks so they know where they are in the movie.

One summer, I worked as the night guard in an office building. It was often a lonely and claustrophobic job, but it was also fascinating to see the inner workings of a high-tech skyscraper – the ventilation shafts, the sophisticated security systems, etc. It was really like a self-contained, little city. And I thought, wouldn't it be cool for an action film to take place in that confined setting?

I had an idea for an R-rated action film about a tough New York City Cop who is accidently trapped inside an LA office building when the building is seized by terrorists. The Cop must evade capture and rescue the hostages, including his wife, armed only with his wits. And I call it "Die Hard."

The story is set almost entirely in a high-rise, high-tech office building in one night. Our hero is John McClane. He's tough as they come but still human. And right now, he's worried about his marriage.

It's Christmas Eve but NYPD cop John travels to LA to patch things up his wife Holly. They've been drifting apart and Holly has recently moved to LA to pursue her promising white-collar career, working for a wealthy Japanese corporation in one of LA's modern, high-rise office buildings.

John meets Holly at her office, where everyone is still working on the day before Christmas. Holly still has feelings for John and admires his integrity, but they are just from different worlds, and she is happy with her new life in LA. John is further disheartened to learn that Holly has reverted to using her maiden name in business. It looks bad for the marriage.

John is frustrated, but it's not in his nature to ever give up. Ever! He wants to talk, but right now Holly is late for her office Christmas party down the hall. While John is cleaning up, he hears shots fired! The building has been seized by a group of well-armed European terrorists, led by mastermind Hans Gruber. Hans takes everyone hostage, including John's wife Holly and her wealthy corporate Boss. With the building locked down, John manages to avoid detection, but he's trapped in the building like everyone else. Which brings us to the end of act one.

John is a good cop, but he's not a super hero, and he immediately calls the LAPD. The LAPD has no evidence of the hostage event and thinks John is making a prank call! But the LAPD sends a lowly Beat Cop around to check it out, just in case. The Beat Cop was on his way home for Christmas Eve, but duty calls. He does a drive-by, but all seems quiet.

Things quickly take a horrible turn when John sees Hans trying to get the lock codes to the company vault from Holly's Boss. When the Boss refuses, Hans executes him in cold blood. John reacts and tries to flee, but this alerts Hans that someone is loose in the building. John narrowly escapes in a hail of automatic gunfire, but now John realizes these "terrorists" are not what they seem. Hans is as deadly as he is brilliant. John knows that if Hans learns that Holly is his wife, she will be in terrible danger!

Frustrated and desperate, John manages to kill one of Hans' crew and is shocked to see the dead guy was carrying a bag of high explosives! John takes the dead guy's radio, but can only reach the Beat Cop. The Beat Cop doesn't believe John either – until, in sheer desperation, John drops the dead guy's body from the 47th floor onto the Cop's patrol car, which leads Hans' crew to destroy what's left of the patrol car with automatic weapons.

Now it's on! The LAPD surrounds the building. John tries to warn the Beat Cop that Hans and his crew are not what they seem and very dangerous. But the FBI has arrived and takes command – the Beat Cop is sympathetic, but powerless. The Feds even think John might be working with the bad guys! John knows it is up to him to save his wife and the others from the inside. John starts a one-man war – killing off Hans' crew, one by one.

The FBI tries to negotiate with Hans, who is just burning time while his team tries to crack the vault code! We now know they are only there for bonds in the safe. John tries to stop them, but by this time he has been bloodied and beat up pretty good, and his only friend in the world is a lowly Beat Cop he's never met.

In act three, John learns that Hans plans to kill all the hostages with a massive explosion as part of a diversion that will allow the terrorists to escape with the bonds. John, taking fire from all sides, manages to save the hostages just before a massive explosion destroys the top of the building. Unfortunately, Hans has learned John's identity and that Holly is his wife. Hans threatens to kill Holly, but John outsmarts Hans, saving Holly. Hans falls 40 stories to his death. It's over.

Bloodied and exhausted John and Holly exit the building... but one terrorist is still alive and still determined to kill John! But at the last moment the terrorist is shot dead in his tracks... by John's lone ally – the lowly Beat Cop – saving John and Holly. It's been a long night for both, but we know that John and Holly will recommit to making their marriage work.

How did we do?

If you know the plot of this film well, you may also notice we altered the presentation of some of the events in the story. For example, the Beat Cop (played by actor Reginald Veljohnson) doesn't come into the film until about 45 minutes into the story, and he doesn't become a significant character until the second half of the film. But in our sample pitch we decided to introduce him earlier, because he is such an important character. We did this because it is sometimes necessary to alter some details to help make them comprehensible to the listener in the abbreviated form of a pitch. This is done for clarity and not to deceive.

Building Out to a Full-Length Pitch.

If you were to expand the five-minute pitch of "Die Hard" to a full-length (10 or 15 minutes) pitch, you would expand the detail in the plot section of the pitch. The personal connection, log line, and character descriptions would remain very similar to the five-minute pitch. Expanding the plot would involve elaborating on the descriptions of the set pieces, describing more of the twists and turns of the plot, and delving deeper into the character's internal journey. You would likely also include descriptions of the subplots that would be left out of shorter pitches, and explanations of some of the secondary characters' internal journeys. As you expand, remember to keep the storytelling relentlessly focused on the characters. The longer the pitch the greater the danger that it falls into a recitation of plot mechanics.

For example, if you were to expand on our "Die Hard" pitch, you might add a description of the scene where John has to run across broken glass in his bare feet (a set piece), include Hans pretending to be an escaped hostage (plot twist), greater detail on John and his wife's marital problems (character journey), and the beat cop's back story of having shot a kid and how he overcomes that fear in the end (subplot).

PITCHING FOR TELEVISION

The business of television has changed dramatically since the late 1990s. What was once the unloved stepchild of the entertainment industry (relative to the movie business) has since blossomed and come into its own. The amazing volume of high quality programming spread across the network, cable and internet universe should be fully appreciated for what it is: a second golden age of television. This is great news for viewers, but it's also great news for writers, producers, and directors whose interests extend to television.

The worldwide television programming landscape is truly vast and diverse, so any attempt to summarize the range of things that are pitched there is doomed to be incomplete, but we will try. Before we get to the specific considerations for pitching television, let's start with an overview of the creative landscape.

The Show-Runner.

Because of the high stakes in television, the job of creating scripted network and cable television series almost always goes to highly experienced writers with long track records of success. The writers at the top of the television food chain, the so-called "show-runners," often spend a decade or more working their way up from the bottom, starting as a staff writer or even the writer's assistant. Want proof? Pick your favorite television series and then look up the prior credits of the series creator or show-runner (always credited as "Executive Producer"). You will probably see a long resume filled with credits like "producer," "consulting producer" or "co-executive producer" – all of which are mid-level writing credits in television.

With so much at stake, networks and cable companies are reluctant to put their trust in anyone without these qualifications. If you are a network or cable executive supervising the production of as many as 22 episodes per series, per season, the thing that keeps you awake at night will be nightmares about scripts not being delivered and shows not completed by scheduled air dates. CBS cannot afford to air a black screen at 9 pm on Thursday. It's hard to overstate how important this is to television companies. The writers who can deliver in these circumstances are highly sought after and lavishly compensated.

Frankly, it is almost impossible for anyone who is not already a well-established writer to sell a series pitch. Considering the enormous demands and deadlines in series television, networks and cable companies are extremely cautious when it comes to deciding what they will develop and produce and whom they will hire to write. This is also one of the reasons why networks and cable companies rarely hire writers to rewrite their series, with the exception being the rewrites performed by members of the writing staff of a series that is in production.

There are some notable exceptions to selling a pitch in this mostly closed world. There have been a few cases where a less established writer has pitched to a well-established show-runner and sold a series idea. This is rare because well-established writers in television typically have plenty of their own ideas and they don't need to share the credit (or money) with anyone. In the rare exception when the series *does* originate with a less-experienced writer, they are typically not in charge of the day-to-day running of the series.

There have also been a few situations where mid-level television writers have sold spec pilots. Yes, we know this is a book about pitching, but remember part of the premise of this book assumes you will be pitching your spec at some point.

Also, many top movie producers have made a foray into series television in the last decade. Jerry Bruckheimer, Steven Spielberg and Mark Gordon are a few names you might recognize, although in most cases they will sell their projects to television with established show-runners attached.

It's also become somewhat common for established feature film writers to sell a television series based on a pitch. (Shonda Rhimes was primarily a feature writer when she sold "Grey's Anatomy.") But like the experienced show-runner, by the time you end up in this situation you will already have had a lot of pitching experience and probably won't need this book.

Where newcomers may have more opportunity is in streaming services and short-form, internet-delivered content. This is because there is typically less pressure to meet a release date. Shows delivered via streaming usually don't follow seasons. And in many cases, these shows are much lower budget than network or cable shows. Niche streaming services like Crackle and Funny or Die, or emerging platforms like Facebook Watch and YouTube Red are more likely to take a chance on inexperienced talent. But even the bigger streaming services will occasionally take a risk. Matt and Ross Duffer had only a few television credits before Netflix bought their series, "Stranger Things." This area of the business is changing rapidly. New "platforms" are appearing practically every month, so following the trade press is particularly important if you pursue this route.

Working in Television.

Most of the pitching tips we've presented so far, and others we will soon discuss, still apply in the process of creating and selling most types of scripted television shows. The primary differences are derived from things like series format and how a series franchise works.

Writers with ambitions in television should fully understand that the workplace lifestyle in television is very different from that of film. Unlike the solitary lifestyle of most movie writers, television writers work in a highly collaborative, highly competitive environment, with brutal deadlines and pressure. While the work hours can be marginally lighter for one-hour drama series, half-hour series writers frequently work incredibly long hours, trying to meet impossible production schedules. The ability to get along with others and manage stress are important requirements in television.

The lifestyle of a television director is also very different, especially in one-hour drama, where the director is often a one-episode "hired gun" for just a few weeks and is usually uninvolved with shaping the series as a whole. We will return to this subject when we discuss director pitches later in the book.

Now let's turn our attention to the specifics of pitching for television.

Franchise.

The approach to constructing a pitch intended as a television series has many of the same challenges as a pitch for a film or television movie, but there are also some very important differences, some of which we've already discussed. The ongoing nature of a television series makes it virtually impossible to pitch based on episodic plots. No television executive expects a writer to come in and pitch 20 to 100 plotlines to sell the show. This point seems even more ridiculous if you analyze any plot line for, say, a typical half-hour sitcom. The plot lines are incredibly slight.

For example, a typical episode log line for the sitcom "The Goldbergs" might be as simple as "Adam tries to convince his grandfather to take him to an R-rated movie." Not much of a story, and no experienced writer would pitch the series based on this type of episodic plot lines. While the plot lines for one-hour drama series are typically more complex, especially for police procedurals like any of the "CSI" series, no writer pitches a one-hour drama idea by summarizing the plots of the ongoing episodes.

Instead of episodic plot, television pitches focus on the types of characters that the audience will want to spend time with every week, the world of the show, and the "engine" that is going to generate stories. The engine of the potential stories is usually referred to as the series "franchise." One of the reasons cop, lawyer, and medical shows have been so common on television is that they have built-in "story engines" that are clear. Every viewer understands what the people in these professions do for a living and therefore what kinds of stories will happen on a weekly basis. In a cop show, a crime is committed, a criminal must be apprehended, and someone's life will be saved. A lawyer will get a new case; the client may or may not be innocent. The guilty are punished. A doctor gets a patient. The patient presents with unusual symptoms. The doctor must race against time to find a cure and save a life. There have been dozens of variations in these well-trod franchises. Series like these can continue, on and on, generating storylines for years, and that's what networks and cable companies are looking for. Of course, not all series have such a clear franchise. For example, how would you describe the series franchise of the hit series "This is Us"? It's really not much more than an unusual family – with a tragic past – working out its issues, week after week.

Open-Ended or Closed-Ended.

Additionally, there are the two basic types of scripted television series – "open-ended" and "closed-ended." Sometimes they are referred to as "serialized" and "procedural," respectively. We prefer the former terms so as not to confuse the series type called procedural with the genre called "procedural," which refers to investigative shows, usually involving cops or detectives. For example, the series "24" is in the procedural genre, but it is also serialized.

In a closed-ended series every episode stands on its own, with minimal on-going storylines. The various incarnations of "Law and Order" are typical of closed-ended series. Most half-hour comedies are closed-ended. Open-ended shows are those with strong ongoing storylines. "The Walking Dead" and "Game of Thrones" are examples of open-ended series, but there are many others.

The easiest way to distinguish between the two forms is to see whether or not the show will make sense to the viewer if the episodes are played out of their original broadcast order. If the series still makes sense, the show is closed-ended. If not, the series is open-ended. Try dropping in on a random episode of the series "Game of Thrones" (a very open-ended series) if you haven't been following the series from the beginning, and you will know exactly what we mean. Indeed, this is why the distinction is so important. If you are pitching a television series, it will be a factor in the buyer's decision whether or not to buy the pitch. Until recently, closed-ended, one-hour drama series were considered more valuable in the marketplace, but in recent years that trend has changed. Because of the declining viewer interest in reruns, and the rise of "binge watching," the trend has shifted to preferring open-ended series for one-hour dramas. Most half-hour scripted comedies remain very closed ended.

Your approach to pitching closed-ended versus open-ended series will vary. For a closed-ended series, you will spend more time describing the arena, the characters, and their conflicts, as a way of explaining where the individual stories will originate, if it's not obvious as it would be in, say, a detective show. You may go through the plot of the pilot (or first episode) as a kind of proto-story or if the pilot is a so-called "premise pilot," a pilot where we see the origination of the premise, or where characters enter an unfamiliar or unique world that will be the basis of the series. ("Lost," or "Designated Survivor" for example.) However, in many closed-ended series pitches, the story of the pilot is barely mentioned. For an open-ended series, it's not unusual to pitch the pilot (especially with premise pilots) and thereafter give an overview of where the story will go throughout the first season, and beyond – the so-called "season arcs." But even here, it is *not* the story of the first episode of the pilot you are trying to sell, it is the story of the entire series.

"GHOST WHISPERER"

by John Gray

In 2004 I was happily toiling away writing and directing fairly high-end movies for broadcast and cable. Many of those movies and mini-series were done for CBS. I had no thoughts about or even desire to do series – I loved the nomadic life of movies, where I could immerse myself in a world and a location for 4 or 5 months and then on to some completely different world and location.

One day, a CBS executive called to ask if I would be interested in a series idea, about a woman she had met through famed psychic James Van Praagh. This woman, known as Mary Ann, could, according to Van Praagh, see the spirits of the dead who had not crossed over. In fact, she could help them cross over. If you were dead and had crossed over, she couldn't see you – but if were dead and still hanging around, she couldn't miss you.

Always loving a good ghost story, I agreed to meet Mary Ann. I was expecting an exotically dressed mysterious woman, probably with a hard to place European accent; what I got was a salt of the earth Midwestern woman with a big infectious smile and an ex-Marine husband with a crew cut, who were about as normal as they come. Just so happens she can see dead people.

While we were sitting in Starbucks, I asked her if she could see any dead people in the vicinity, and she proceeded to clue me in to the presence of at least 3 ghosts right there in Starbucks, and why they were still there, and what they needed in terms of closure to cross over (I ended up putting this scene in the pilot).

As I drove away, I felt very strongly that I wanted to, that I could, make a series out of this. I love the horror genre, and I love strong character driven drama. Here was a chance to fuse both. I also saw it as a chance to work out some of my own feelings and fears about death, closure, and redemption. I think it's important in anything you pitch to have a personal component, even if it's hidden, that resonates with you and is something you'll want to keep exploring. Without that I think you make a much harder road for yourself. I told CBS I was interested.

Now, it was up to me to come up with a take for the show, a way into the world, who the main characters would be, and what the template of the show would be on a weekly basis.

My producing partners, Ian Sander and Kim Moses, and I spent about a month or so shaping and developing the show. My feeling was to center it on a normal young woman, just starting out, who, in spite of this gift (curse?) of being able to deal with the dead, is just trying to have a life, get married, start a business, like anyone else. Her constant conflict would be whether she could in good conscience ignore the spirits around her who need her help. Each episode would begin as a mini-horror movie, then evolve into the mystery of what the ghost needed to cross over. I anticipated a several-episode arc during which the main character would agonize over whether she should tell her fiancé/new husband about the fact that she sees dead people.

My first pitch was to CBS, since of course the idea originated there. I felt obligated to go there first. By the time I went in for the pitch, I had worked out the world of the story, who the main characters were, how the guest cast would come in and out of each episode, the tone of the show, and what the template of each episode would be – the appearance of a ghost, the mystery surrounding its presence, procedural beats to solve the mystery, the main character discovering what particular piece of closure is needed to send the spirit on its way, resolution.

Because what's most important to the network is not so much the pilot, but how the <u>series</u> will work and stay fresh for a season, and hopefully 5 seasons, I actually don't spend too much time on the pilot itself in a pitch. I happen to love pitching, I love storytelling, and I look at pitching as a piece of performance art. My job is to get the listeners to forget where they are and what they were doing before and what they have to do later and get them totally lost in the story and the characters. They have to feel my passion for it. And pitching the <u>characters</u> is crucial, because that's what keeps the audience coming back week after week. Doesn't matter how great your plots are, how clever your gimmick is, if you don't love the people (or at least be fascinated by them) you have nothing. So I spend a lot of time (relative to the whole pitch) painting pictures of the characters and what makes them unique and why we can't wait to spend time with them every week.

Over the years, I guess I've come up with a way of pitching series that I'm most comfortable with and seems to be effective. The way I start (after the obligatory small talk and traffic complaints) is to jump into the teaser of the pilot – I make sure it's arresting, visual, and compelling – and gives us a good sense of what the main character is like – and I end it on a cliffhanger. I then leave them hanging, as it were, and step back and talk in a broader sense about the series, the world, the characters. I try to use examples of random episodes that give a good feeling for the direction the show will take, and the potential for the growth of the characters. I try to show the entire palette of the show; a quick example of how it will be scary, how it will be mysterious, how it will be funny. I like throwing out bits and pieces of dialog. I talk about the visual look of the show; and how we will use music.

It's also good to come armed with research or some other visual aids. My producing partners came prepared with some pretty compelling audience research about the growing fascination at the time with all things supernatural, and some interesting box office figures for the most recent horror movies. The sad truth is, more often than not, executives are mostly looking for a reason to say no. This keeps them safe, at least for a time. You have to provide so many overwhelming reasons to make them feel <u>safe</u> saying yes, that even the most frightened executive will feel comfortable going forward.

One of the last things I'll do is give at least 3 brief loglines for additional episodes. Once I've made it through all of the above, if I still feel the room is warm and I haven't overstayed my welcome, I'll come back to the pilot and finish the pitch on what happens and how it ends. However, if I feel the pitch has gone really well, and everyone is feeling good, I'll leave well enough alone. I think it's important to know when to quit while you're ahead.

I think it was just a day or two later that we got the call – CBS was buying the pitch and I would start writing the pilot. This was a great feeling and there was an hour and a half or so of celebrating, then the next network call comes which tells you exactly what pilot the network wants, which may not be the pilot you thought you sold. In our case, CBS had told us they loved the fact that they didn't have any other shows like this on the air; but in the development process they slowly but surely made sure it looked like nearly every show they had on the air in terms of it being a procedural; the solving of a mystery became the central focus of each episode. They also felt strongly that we should go into the pilot with the husband of the main character already being fully aware of her abilities. I fought hard against this; to me this was taking away a huge conflict for the main character, and we all know that thing about conflict equals drama etc. I lost that battle, and many more – but I can't fault CBS in any way – they know what works for their audience and under the CBS template the show lasted for 5 years, always winning its time slot, even in its last season, and almost always winning the night. The trick is learning to work within a network's parameters and still make it personal and satisfying to you.

Set Pieces.

Unlike feature films, there is little or no emphasis on specific set pieces when pitching television. The limited budgets and production schedules in television make elaborately produced sequences tough to pull off. That said, there are some television series that proudly cultivate something equivalent to set pieces: "water cooler moments." A water cooler moment is a provocative or shocking sequence in a television show that will inspire viewers to discuss it the next day at the office, presumably while they're standing around the water cooler. Series that are famous for their water cooler moments include "Seinfeld," "Curb Your Enthusiasm," or really any series on Showtime. The HBO series "Game of Thrones" has been inspiring water cooler chatter by killing off major characters on a regular basis. Other series have been doing the same, if only for a shocking season finale.

Pitching Television Movies.

The television format pitch most similar to a feature film pitch would be a pitch for a television movie. In fact, some television movies start out as motion picture projects before ending up on television. As we said before, ad-supported television movies frequently use a seven-act structure that coincides with a commercial break roughly every fifteen minutes. And it wouldn't be unusual to pitch a television movie by delineating all seven acts. The trick to doing so is finding a small "cliffhanger" in your story every fifteen minutes or so. The purpose of these cliffhangers is to make sure the viewer will want to come back to the story after the commercial break, instead of switching to another channel. Almost all commercial television formats use this technique, not just television movies, and when the scripts are written, the writer will indicate the act breaks. Commercial-free television movies for premium cable, like HBO, typically are pitched in three acts, just like feature films. In most television movie scripts intended for outlets that do not use commercials, the writer will *not* indicate act breaks.

Pitching One-Hour Drama and Half-Hour Comedy Series.

The success of most series relies upon the audience's willingness to get wrapped up in the lives of the characters on a long-term basis. So your series pitch should spend more time elaborating the details of the characters' lives, personalities and pasts, even though the details of those lives may take many seasons of episodes to be revealed. Because of the added details required, the description of your main characters will most likely not be incorporated into the body of your plot, if plot is pitched at all.

Describing the proscenium of the series is not that different from one format to another. Sometimes, the proscenium of your series is very closely related to the franchise of your series. If you're pitching a medical series, the main setting will likely be a hospital. If it's a cop show, the main setting might be the precinct. The limited budgets in television will require you to spend much of the series using the handful of locations or sets built for the series. Keep this in mind when you construct your series pitch. It will surely be on the mind of your listener.

Animation.

For writers, pitching animation works very much like pitching live action. You construct a pitch for an animated feature film exactly like you construct a pitch for a live action film. Similarly, pitching an episode idea for an existing animated television series is exactly like pitching an episode idea for a live action series (and like live action series, many shows do not use freelance writers).

When it comes to pitching an idea for a new television series, things are a little different. In the animation world, artists can be more involved in the process. Pitches are often accompanied by concept art showing the characters, the world, and the visual style and tone of the story. Still, you don't need an artist to pitch an original animated series. Executives often have artists that they want to team up with writers. But if you have an artist or art skills, and a strong vision of the visuals for your show, artwork never hurts.

What is Reality?

This book spends a lot of time talking about pitching films, scripted television series and television movies. But there's another entire universe of programming that gets pitched in Hollywood: so-called "reality" series. Reality series (sometimes called "unscripted" series) are a vast and diverse subset of television programming that includes things like cooking shows, celebrity shows, "docu-soaps," competition shows, real estate shows, makeover shows, travel shows, and many more subset categories. Some recent examples include "The Real Housewives of Beverly Hills," "American Idol," "America's Next Top Model," "Shark Tank," "Keeping Up with the Kardashians," "Property Brothers," "Judge Judy," "Dance Moms," "Chopped," and many more. Although similar programming has been around since the early days of television, the proliferation of cable channels in the last fifteen or twenty years, combined with the low cost of reality production, has led to an explosion of this type of programming. Now, all major networks and television production companies develop reality programming, although they usually prefer to call it "unscripted."

Whether or not some reality series are truly unscripted (as in "no writers employed") is a hotly debated topic in Hollywood. This is especially true within the Writers Guild of America, which has more than a little skin in the game when it comes to this issue. But it's also true that many series that are called reality series *are* written and *have* writers credited on their episodes.

In any case, reality series are typically not the kinds of series that writers pitch. More often than not, it is a producer doing the pitching. Ambitious filmmakers should know that pitching ideas for reality programming has some unique aspects, but also quite a lot of opportunity because of the huge volume of programming. Before we discuss the specifics of pitching reality series, let's try to get on the same page about what they are. Because of the diversity of this kind of television programming, any attempt to generalize is likely doomed to paint an incomplete picture. With that caveat, what do some of the above shows have in common?

First of all, while some of these series may not employ individuals credited as writers, to call all of these series "reality" is a little misleading. Many of these shows have a highly-constructed series format: the "real" people who appear in these series are "cast," the story scenarios within the episodes are typically created by the series' producers, and what you end up watching is always the result of a well-considered editorial process, soundtrack and all. And sometimes dialogue is even given to the stars of these shows, and multiple takes are done of the "real" events. For this reason, the word "reality" is not always the best description. If you want reality, maybe try CNN.

Second, for the personality-driven shows, the rules of character and drama still apply just as they would with scripted programming. While the people you are watching are real people, to the viewers they are characters, just as much as if it were a soap opera – and some of these shows come pretty close to playing exactly like soap operas. Often, there are good guys and bad guys, conflicts, and dramatic situations. For a personality-driven reality series – no drama, no show.

Lastly, all of these series exist on a continuum based on how planned-out the storylines are when they are shot. They range from semi-documentary style, where the camera crew follows people as they live their lives ("Keeping Up with the Kardashians," "Little Women: LA") to semi-scripted shows ("Bobby Flay's Barbecue Addiction," "Impractical Jokers") to heavily formatted series ("American Idol," "The Bachelor") where people are put into contrived situations, complete with known rules and defined structure.

There's another kind of programming that gets grouped with reality programming, but is probably more accurately described as "documentary," or "docuseries" programming. This includes shows like "Making a Murderer," "The Vietnam War," "Anthony Bourdain: Parts Unknown" and "30 for 30." All of these series are semi-scripted. Each episode is really a mini documentary.

Despite the diversity of reality programming, the way these series get pitched is not all that different than pitching scripted series. In a reality pitch, things like personal connection, tone, log line, characters, and plot all have an equivalent, with a few notable differences:

First, many reality shows are personality driven, meaning that in most cases you will need to have a famous actor, expert, celebrity, or unusual "real" people involved before you pitch. How would you pitch a series like "Keeping Up with the Kardashians" without having the Kardashian family attached to the project? What would be the appeal of "Real Housewives" if you didn't know anything about the housewives who were going to be featured?

"American Idol" depends heavily on celebrity judges and cooking shows are dependent on the chef's personality. Though common, it is not *uniformly* true that all reality series must have a cast in place for a successful pitch. For example, "Ancient Aliens," "Bible Rules," and perhaps even "Shark Tank" might be pitched without an actor, real person, celebrity, or successful entrepreneur (in the case of "Shark Tank") attached.

Second, the centerpiece of almost all unscripted series pitches will be a short audio/video presentation. Whereas most film and scripted television series pitches do *not* involve this component (see our later chapter on "Props and Leave-behinds"), most reality and non-fiction shows will incorporate an A/V presentation, also known as a "sizzle reel." A sizzle reel is a lively and heavily edited 3 to 5-minute promotional video presentation that is used to excite buyers and help them visualize the potential of the series. For reality pitches, sizzle reels are often used to convey specific locations, characters, storylines, dramatic conflicts, and other aspects specific to a particular series. Hopefully, the reason for this is obvious: If you're pitching something that's "real," it's important for the buyer to see the real thing that exists. In many cases, a reel (sometimes called a "deck") will be presented first, followed by a verbal pitch – like the one that follows – that more fully explains the premise, the characters, and the franchise of the show. There are numerous examples of sizzle reels for (mostly unsold) reality and non-fiction series on Vimeo and YouTube, some of them are very professionally produced.

Last, there are some additional conventions when pitching reality series that are a little different. For example, you are more likely to use comparisons to similar series ("It's 'West Coast Customs' meets "Fixer Upper'"). Also, the use of taglines is more common ("Got a dream? They can build it"). These differences are modest and just a matter of industry custom.

Sample Reality Pitch

Here is an outline for an unscripted series pitch called "Dream Wheels." You will see some similarities with the examples we gave you for a film or scripted series pitch. We will leave the section headings in so you can see the similarities. The actual pitch would likely be about ten minutes, so this is only an outline and does not include everything that would actually be said in the room.

Personal Connection

Everyone knows the food truck business is on fire. But food trucks are just the tip of the iceberg. A truck can be customized to suit almost any kind of mobile business you can imagine. All over America, entrepreneurs are finding these vehicles are the key to making their dreams come true: Hair & makeup salons, mobile masseuses, manicurists, florists, personal training and pet grooming, to name a few. And compared to starting a brick and mortar business, the cost-to-entry for a mobile business can be less than a tenth the cost. Plus, if business is bad in one spot, you can just drive to a new location and set up shop. The name of this show is...

Title

"Dream Wheels"

Log Line

It's 'West Coast Customs' meets 'Fixer Upper.' A successful husband and wife team run LA Custom Trailers, building the coolest custom trucks for mobile businesses. Together with their team of talented builders, they make dreams come true for young entrepreneurs starting their own mobile businesses.

Genre/Tone

A 30-minute docu-series. Inspirational and sometimes funny.

Tagline

Got a dream? They can build it.

Characters

The series focuses on married couple Susan and Charlie, the owners of LA Custom Trailers.

Located in downtown Los Angeles, LA Custom Trailer is one of the busiest high-end service truck builders in the U.S. For over 14 years, the attractive, dynamic husband and wife team of Susan and Charlie have grown their custom truck business by building the best custom trucks for every need. Don't be fooled by their glamorous looks and affluent Calabasas lifestyle; Susan and Charlie know how to roll up their sleeves and push their crew of designers and fabricators to build the kinds of trucks that are sold to both Fortune 500 companies and people just staring out in business. They make a great team. But more than this, Susan and Charlie care about the people who walk in their door. After all, they're not just building a truck, they're taking someone's dream job and making it a reality.

...A shrewd MBA, Susan runs the front office, dealing with clients. Part business-woman, part lifestyle guru, her job is to take the clients dreams and career aspirations and figure out how to make them a reality, while staying within a budget. Charlie, by contrast, spends more of his time working with the LACT crew of builders – a group known as much for their relentless pranks as their expert construction. But don't let Charlie's affable, blue-collar nature fool you: he has a degree in automotive engineering from ArtCenter College of Design. He could be working for Honda but wanted to start his own business instead. All this contributes to a mostly upbeat and light-hearted work environment. But when problems arise, it will be Susan, as much as Charlie, who has to bust some heads and get the job done...

And so on. This section might run five to seven paragraphs and might also include short "character" sketches of the colorful supporting crew of fabricators that work at LACT, although they would also surely be featured in the sizzle reel created for the pitch.

The Franchise

The series will mostly focus on a 'build a week' at work and the contrasting upscale Calabasas lifestyle of Susan and Charlie.

Each episode will feature a new customer who dreams of starting a new business or expanding an existing business. One custom dream truck will be built in each episode...

...Susan and Charlie will consult with the entrepreneur and try to make their dreams wheels a reality by reconciling their dream <u>with</u> reality. Often the entrepreneur will be inexperienced and Susan and Charlie will have to "school" a client with an unrealistic business plan. And of course, it's not easy building something that's never been built before...

...Each episode will intercut between the LACT team building a custom truck and a profile of the new customer who ordered it..."

And so on. This section might also run five to seven paragraphs. The goal is to capture a sense of the characters, what will drive each story, and where the challenges, conflict and drama will come from on a weekly basis.

Keep in mind that this sample series pitch is fairly closed-ended. Each episode features one build and there are minimal continuing storylines. Other kinds of series might have more of an ongoing narrative, for example, a series like "Survivor" or "Big Brother." If you are pitching a more open-ended series, your pitch would surely want to capture a sense of how the series would unfold over the course of season. If there are rules and structure to the series, you will want to make that clear.

You might notice that the above sample pitch features several possible storylines, and this is intentional. This is because different potential buyers will want to emphasize different aspects of the series. For example, A&E might want to emphasize the luxurious Calabasas lifestyle and its contrast with Susan and Charlie's working-class business. Velocity would surely be more interested in the details of the builds and the fabricators, and

CNBC more interested in the "entrepreneur of the week" aspect. The point is to leave yourself enough options in your pitch so as to make the series most marketable to the widest variety of buyers. A shrew producer pitching this series will tweak their pitch, depending on the buyer.

PITCHING REWRITES OR ADAPTATIONS

> "Acting is all about honesty. If you can fake that, you've got it made.
> -George Burns

The most common type of pitch meeting for a writer in feature films (and occasionally television) is one where the project being pitched is a rewrite or adaptation of something that is based on "assigned material." Assigned material is any preexisting intellectual property ("I.P.") that didn't originate with the writer (or director, or producer, etc.). Examples of assigned material are other writer's scripts, books, plays, true stories, comic books, and remakes or sequels of an existing film or television show. There are some specific considerations you should incorporate when pitching a rewrite or adaptation that's based on assigned material. Many of the same considerations also apply if you are a film director pitching your take to get hired. But for now, we will use a writer's pitch as our example.

It is not unusual for multiple writers to rewrite studio scripts before they are produced. There are plenty of projects that have had over a dozen writers reworking a script before the film is made. We are not saying this is a good way to create movies, but it is the reality of Hollywood. Consequently, most of the writing jobs are rewrites of existing scripts rather than something a writer will develop from scratch.

There is also a pervasive belief in Hollywood that basing a film or television project on a recognizable preexisting property will increase its chance of success, so adaptations tend to be given higher regard than original ideas. Plus, success in another medium validates the story, which in turn validates an executive's decision to invest in it. In order to get these types of jobs, you will have to pitch "your take" on the source material.

Three side-notes before we continue:

First, the rewriting scenario does not apply to series television, where rewrite assignments are virtually nonexistent, except for the rewriting done by the writers on the series' writing staff. Rewrites of "long form" television are more common. Long form includes television movies and mini-series (also known as limited series). However, since television series are often based on underlying material – "The Handmaid's Tale," "Game of Thrones," "Supergirl" and "Jessica Jones," for example – a pitch for this kind of show will use the techniques discussed in this chapter.

Second, it is entirely possible that you might pitch a project that is based on some existing intellectual property that you either originated or control. This would be the case if (for example) you want to pitch an adaptation of a play or novel *you* wrote, or some other source material you did not originate but where you have the right to adapt that source material – maybe a book you optioned, or maybe you found something cool in the public domain. These kinds of situations do arise, but a pitch of this kind is performed almost exactly like an original idea *unless* for some reason your listener is very familiar with the underlying material you want to adapt. This situation also happens, and it's great when it does, assuming your listener likes your underlying material. If your listener is familiar with the underlying material you own or control, you would then pitch the project along the lines presented in this chapter.

Lastly, if you control the rights to the underlying material for a project you are pitching, this situation does *not* involve *assigned* material, though it is still an adaptation.

Analyzing the Material and Personal Connection.

When pitching a project based on assigned material, the significant differences in approach will lie in your analysis of the source material and the approach to your personal connection.

The analysis of the source material is required because you are pitching changes to something that already exists. The way you justify these changes is by analyzing and articulating what works and doesn't work in the underlying material. Notice we didn't use the words "good" and "bad." You're not pitching as an art critic; you're pitching to get a job.

The difference in the personal connection is required because (in most cases) you won't have a personal connection based on your origination of the project.

Both of these differences in approach require an extra degree of sophistication, and this is one of the reasons that professional "script doctors" tend to be amongst the highest paid writers in Hollywood.

A full presentation of script and story analysis is beyond the scope of this book, but here are a few helpful suggestions for how to approach your analysis and personal connection in this kind of pitching situation.

Personal Connection.

If you're trying to get hired as a writer or director on an assignment, start by learning what you can about the history of the project. It's usually not a secret. You might be able to read about the underlying material online on one of the trade publications' websites. Frequently when a project is acquired, there will be a news article that discusses the project, and why the buyer liked it. Often, you can get some feedback from the studio, network or producer about what they like and don't like, and what direction they'd like to go. But regardless, your analysis of the existing material will show what you bring to the table. This is a major part of your "take." It's the reason they should hire you instead of one of the hundreds of other experienced professional writers or directors who want a job.

Most pitches based on assigned material should start off with a personal connection. As we said, because you didn't originate the project, your personal connection can't be based on the project origins. This doesn't mean it is impossible to incorporate a personal element here. If your father read you the novel as a child, you may have a unique perspective on the themes of the story. Or maybe the subject of the underlying material reminds you of an experience you had while you were serving in the military. If you can establish a legitimate personal connection to the material, it will go a long way to establishing why you are a good candidate for the assignment.

Be specific. If you just say, "This was my favorite comic book when I was a kid," they'll probably assume you're just blowing smoke to get the job. And who cares if the main character is just like your uncle Sal if your relationship with your uncle doesn't influence your approach to the story in some way? Like the personal connection in an original story, any personal connection used for an assignment should set up what you're going to propose later in the pitch.

Let's look at an example of how you might craft a personal connection for a potential assignment. Imagine you are going

Pitching Rewrites or Adaptations

into a meeting to pitch your adaptation of Michael Crichton's novel "Jurassic Park." You might begin with:

"I grew up watching science fiction movies and I've seen every Godzilla movie ever made. That's why I think I'm the right person to adapt this book."

This is an okay way to start. It's certainly a plus that you would be familiar with the genre. However, it's likely that every other writer going up for this job will also be an aficionado of science fiction. This personal connection is simply not "personal" enough. It is also a little too superficial and risks sounding desperate. Let's try again.

"My personal connection is that I have always been fascinated by the contradictions of science. Take nuclear fission. The men who mastered the atom were also the men that brought about the creation of the nuclear bomb. There is a dark side to the advancement of human knowledge. This is the theme I'd like to explore in adapting 'Jurassic Park.'"

The idea here is good, but again it's not very personal. Moreover, both of these two examples lack grace. They feel too formal, like a high school class presentation. Articulating the words "my personal connection" is a little too "how I spent my summer vacation." Here's an example that is both more elegant and more personal:

"I was a child during the cold war, and I vividly remember the drills where we had to hide under our desks as some kind of ridiculous protection in the event of a nuclear attack. Living in constant fear of nuclear war, I was naturally fascinated that many of the men who developed the bomb questioned the morality of their work. Yet good things came out of that work as well – nuclear energy and scientific advancement that we've built upon since then. This was on my mind as I read 'Jurassic Park.' The book perfectly captures the struggle between what's possible, and what's right. But instead of nuclear bombs, we have Tyrannosaurs Rex."

Pretty good. From there, it would be easy to slide right into a discussion of how you would bring the book to the screen emphasizing those themes of advancement and responsibility.

Another example:

Let's say you were pitching to get the job to write an adaptation of Marvel Comics' "Captain America." You're not a superhero and you probably didn't fight in World War II. Instead, you might start talking about how you were always small for your age and were always picked last for sports, even though you loved sports. You could talk about how you relate to that aspect of Steve Rogers' character – how his desire to serve his country is confounded by his physical limitations.

The personal connection should contextualize the pitch to come. If you were doing the "Captain America" pitch with the take described above, you would want to make certain to reference back to that outsider/weakling theme regularly.

There are other ways into a personal connection for a project like "Captain America." Maybe you have always struggled with the balance between patriotism and the need to hold leaders accountable. Or maybe you are interested in the personal vs. public nature of heroism. The point is that you need to find a way to make the story your own while also serving the take you are about to pitch. Writers frequently take a lot of liberty when they formulate their personal connections for assignments. Sometimes it's entirely faked. We encourage you to do it right: tell the truth, and you'll have it made.

Analysis.

The next step is to analyze the material and figure out what will be required to turn it into a great screenplay, film, or series. We recommend you start your analysis with a broad look at what is appealing and positive in the underlying material. This first step is important: If you hate the underlying material, and say so in the meeting, you are unlikely to get the job. Nor should you have been there in the first place! If you are there to pitch a rewrite or adaptation of someone else's project, it's a pretty good bet the studio or production company likes the project, even if it needs some work. Stay positive and upbeat. Your enthusiasm should always *validate* the listener's decision to have developed the project in the first place.

After accentuating the positive, give a short description of your vision for the project. Do you see this as a story about a man consumed by revenge, or a story of justice gone awry? Is it the story of a cynical woman finding hope, or the story of two moral people leaning on each other in a hostile world? This is the equivalent of the log line in an original pitch, except in this case the listener already knows the idea. You are giving them a premise or through-line to organize what will come later. Make sure it sounds exciting and appealing – you are painting an image of the movie that could be made.

In some instances, you may need to give an actual log line that contains the story concept. This is required when you are adapting material without an obvious plot, such as some non-fiction works. Or if you're adapting a long running television show or comic book series, you have to identify which story you are going to tell among all the options. Even if you are going to tell the origin story, there may have been several versions and you have to identify which one you plan to do.

Sometimes, particularly with adaptations, you have to describe some of the challenges in the existing material before giving this "log line." For example, you may have to point out that, "the problem with the play is that it all takes place in one location, which is not very filmic," before you pitch your idea to turn it into a road movie. Although usually it's best to save any negative analysis until you've clearly established your positive vision for the project.

Rewrites.

If you are pitching a rewrite, at some point you will have to discuss what doesn't work in the last draft. As we said, the first rule of pitching rewrites and adaptations is to avoid insulting the material – even if it's really bad. Even if they tell you they know it's really bad. Of course, the listener knows there are flaws in the existing material – that's why you're there. It is okay to acknowledge the flaws, but be careful! If you over-emphasize what's bad, they may just decide to drop the whole thing – and that means no job for you!

If you're pitching a rewrite of an existing screenplay, insulting the previous draft and/or writer (it's basically the same thing) is considered unprofessional. You know, "Do unto others…" and all that. Again, the person you're pitching to thought that previous writer was good enough that he gave them the job. Are you questioning the producer's taste?

You also don't know the development history. So before you say something like, "It was foolish to try to shoehorn a romance into this action movie," remember that the person sitting across from you may have been the one who suggested adding a romance in the first place. You should assume any insult you lob at the current screenplay is an insult to the person you are hoping will give you the job, so phrase your critique accordingly. Your attitude should be that everyone who has worked on the project so far has helped move it forward, but you are here to bring it all home.

We are not encouraging anyone to lie in this situation. You should always pitch from a place of conviction and honesty. We believe that honesty is the best policy in the long run. This is also the best foundation for a long term working relationship in Hollywood. So, what's the solution? Reassure the buyer that what they have given you to evaluate is filled with potential – potential *you* will realize. Rather than focusing on all the bad things, focus on what you will do to make the script great. So instead of saying, "The character is one-dimensional," say, "I want to make the character more complex and compelling so the audience is really moved when they make the big decision in Act Three." The goal is to get the buyer excited, not discourage them.

As we said earlier, it may be possible to learn in advance why the buyer got involved with the project in the first place. This information can come from your agent or the buyer. If you are handed something to look at in a meeting, ask what they like and don't like. They may not tell you, but it won't hurt to ask. If you can't get straightforward direction, we strongly urge you to do your homework and learn what you can. Here's a trick: sometimes the initial development of a project is announced in the Hollywood trade publications. These announcements are typically accompanied by a project description. Search for the project description in the announcements on the trade press websites. No matter how bad the script they handed you to rewrite, it's possible that what the buyer liked about the original script or idea is described in the announcement.

Once you've analyzed the original material and presented your concise vision, you will most likely walk through your proposed story changes in a linear fashion. Of course, the buyers already know the plot. However, they may or may not know it intimately. You may find yourself pitching to the producer and a couple of studio executives. Maybe the producer and one of the executives have been working closely with the writer of the previous draft, but the other executive only read it once, months ago. Invariably, that person will be the one who decides whether you get the job, so do not let them become confused! That said, you should focus your attention mostly on the things you'll change and skim quickly through the other parts of the plot. These pitches tend to be a little less formal and more conversational and interactive. That's good. Listen carefully to what the buyer says – it will give you clues as to what they hope you will deliver.

Adaptations.

If the assigned material is a book or other literary property, the process is much the same. You will need to spend a fair amount of time analyzing the source material for its strengths and weaknesses and explain how you will translate it to film. This last part is very important. There are many literary works that are challenging to adapt for film or television. It's possible the literary work has little or no action, or that much of the pleasure of the work derives from what's in the main character's head. If the assigned material is a play, the challenge will be how you're going to open it up and make it more filmic. With a newspaper or magazine article, you may have to impose a plot on something that's really more of an arena than a story. Screenwriters who are good at adaptations can carve out a lucrative niche career for themselves.

Sequels, prequels and remakes are another source of great jobs for writers. And once again, the process is much the same as with other assigned material. The catch is that sequels, prequels, and remakes are typically highly valued properties, and it's common for these jobs to go to a writer with a proven track record.

There's one last aspect of assignment pitches we should mention. In addition to the challenges you will face convincing someone of the value of your original idea, there are many situations where the buyer is skeptical about the value of their *own* project. This may sound strange, but it happens all the time with assignments.

Many projects at studios and production companies languish for years without ever finding a writer with a take that works. It's not unusual in this situation for a buyer to see his or her own project as unsolvable. Often this is how new writers get their first job – by pitching a solution to a near-dead project. Other times the buyer might have a bare notion of a subject matter or arena (maybe something set during Spring Break) but they have no idea how to approach it. In both of these examples, part of the writer's task will be to convince the buyer of the value of the buyer's own project. The solution to this task may live or die in your passion and personal connection to the project.

Producers and Directors

We've said repeatedly that this book is not just intended for writers. Anyone who wants to work in the Hollywood creative community will be called upon to pitch their projects, their ideas, and themselves, including producers and directors. If you're just starting out, and want to be a producer or director, we're hoping this is already self-evident. If you *are* an established producer or director, well, it's hard to imagine how you got there without acquiring a great appreciation for the things we teach in this book.

Although we have discussed the way a writer should present a full-length pitch, it's less common that a director or producer will be called upon to deliver a pitch in exactly this way. This doesn't mean that producers and directors don't also pitch – of course they do. But unlike writers, who mostly pitch *stories* for film and television, producers and directors usually pitch from a broader perspective, with less emphasis on the plot or story elements of a pitch and more emphasis on other aspects of film and television production. Producers try to sell their projects. Directors try to sell their services on various projects.

Let's consider some of the different elements a producer or director will routinely incorporate into their pitching, and why. You will see that there is sometimes an overlap between how writers, directors, and producers pitch, but also how the unique job responsibilities of directing and producing require other special considerations.

The Producer Pitch.

There are many kinds of producers in Hollywood, so first let's try to explain whom we are referring to in this section of the book. It's not easy. Unlike the writer and director credits on most Hollywood productions, producer credits are not regulated by a guild or anyone else. A producer credit is a negotiated credit. This makes it hard to tell which producer did what on any given project, based solely on their screen credit. Amazingly, there were 41 producer credits on "Lee Daniels' The Butler." Is it possible all 41 people produced the film? Of course not, but this example illuminates the problem we have when trying to define what a producer does and how they pitch.

First, let's cross a few off the list. We're not talking about line producers, who are responsible for hiring and managing the crew and the day-to-day supervision of budget and schedule. We're not talking about writer/producers in television. They will pitch as any writer would – they will pitch story. There are also manager/producers, who sometimes act like agents, but sometimes like producers. Often financiers will be given Executive Producer credit, however it is more likely they were on the receiving end of the pitch. Confused yet?

The kinds of producers we are talking about are sometimes referred to as "creative producers," but this can also be misleading, and no established producer is ever credited this way. For the sake of simplicity, we will consider the role of the producer based not on credit but rather as it is popularly understood: the person in Hollywood who is supposed to shepherd a project from start to finish, supervising all facets of its creation.

Producers pitch projects all the time. Unlike writers, who may only pitch sporadically (not including writer/producers on series staff), it's not unusual for producers to spend a good chunk of their day selling their wares – pitching their projects, trying to get them made. Sometimes producers will pitch to buyers in conjunction with a writer – and we will discuss that situation very soon – but typically a producer will perform the bulk of their pitching solo – via telephone, in their office.

Here are a few typical pitching scenarios for producers:

- Pitching a script, book, comic, remake, or some other IP to a film or television executive to get them to read it.
- Pitching a project to a Studio to set a meeting so a writer can pitch the project.
- Pitching an open writing or directing assignment to an agent who represents writers or directors.
- Pitching an idea for a film or television project to a writer to get them interested in pitching or writing it.
- Pitching a project to directors or actors to get them attached to a project.
- Pitching a project to an investor to get them to finance it.
- Pitching to a distributor to get them interested in viewing or "picking up" a finished film for distribution.
- Pitching a non-fiction, reality, or unscripted series.

As we said earlier, producers usually spend less time pitching plot and more time pitching other aspects of a project. The three exceptions would be: 1) A producer pitching one of his or her own ideas to a writer, where more plot detail is required because most writers care about such detail. 2) A producer pitching a reality series. Producers typically pitch reality series without a writer, requiring the producer to pitch the additional story details. And 3) a pitch of opportunity where a producer might encounter someone unexpectedly and is called upon to pitch on the spot, without the chance to bring the writer along.

Most producer pitches will run two minutes or less and include title, genre/tone, and log line, at which point the producer will present additional aspects of the project. What are these additional aspects? It will often include several of the following things, when relevant to the listener:

- The history of the project, how the producer got involved with the story, and why the producer is passionate about the material.
- If there's a writer involved, what are his or her other notable credits?
- The pedigree of the project: Is it based on well-known underlying material or has it been associated with well-known talent, for example.
- Any other attachments, such as actors, directors, or other producers.
- The actors or directors that might be right for the project at some point.
- Estimates of how the project will perform in foreign markets. (Foreign accounts for over 50% of revenue for many American films and television shows.)
- The proposed budget for the project.
- What financing is in place, and from whom.
- What rights are available? What deals are already in place?
- What niche the project will fill in the marketplace and who will want to see it.
- Other examples of similar successful projects.
- The programming "hole" that the project will fill in a Network or Cable Company's schedule. Is it a family-friendly, primetime comedy? A 10PM adult, police drama?

Some of these things might be pitched as part of the producer's personal connection, as they would with a writer's pitch. However, many times they will come later, after the log line.

Lastly, let's talk about the interplay that occurs if a producer and writer are pitching a project together. When this happens, the writer will usually be expected to present a full-length pitch to a buyer with the intention of selling it, resulting in getting the writer paid to write a film script, television pilot, rewrite, or adaptation.

In this scenario, a producer will usually be there to support the writer's efforts, enhancing the pitch with some of the additional information listed above, but usually presented either before or after the writer's part of the pitch. When it comes to the story, the producer will usually let the writer speak. This is what the buyer wants to hear. It will be the writer, after all, who will execute the story on the page. It's rare that a producer will interrupt the writer's pitch unless the writer misspeaks or forgets to mention an important story point. (Pitching is hard – it happens.)

You might notice that some of the elements of a producer's pitch overlap with things we said a writer might pitch in the personal connection section of their pitch. For example, a writer pitching alone might mention comparable films or what actors might be ideal for the roles. When a producer and writer pitch together, it would be customary that the producer takes responsibility for pitching these aspects. If the producer and writer have developed the project together, they should work out in advance who will say what during the meeting.

The Director Pitch.

The director is a key member of any Hollywood production team. A director is responsible for the artistic supervision of many, if not most, aspects of film and television production. So of course, many of these aspects will play a part in a director pitch. Directors are not pitching the story so much as their vision of how that story will be realized on film (unless they are also the writer or are pitching their story notes for proposed script changes to support their overall vision). Here is a list of typical director pitching scenarios:

- A director pitches a project with a writer.
- A director pitches their take on a film project to a financier or producer to get hired as the film's director.
- A director pitches a project to a movie star to get them involved in a project, or to get the star to approve the director for a studio project.
- A director pitches their take to a show-runner of a television series to get hired to direct the pilot or an episode of the series.

- A director pitches their take (and budget) on a commercial script (called a board) to get hired to direct the ad.

As you can see from the list above, most of these scenarios involve the director trying to get hired. Only the first example implies the director is originating a project, and even then, the director will be expected to make the case for how they would approach the project as the director.

Of course, there are many cases where a director's pitch will also incorporate suggested changes to the project's script. This is especially true in motion pictures, where it is often an expectation of the director. But unless the director plans to write the script revision, the director's pitch will usually stick to the broader stokes of proposed script changes. If hired, the director will then supervise the existing writer, hire a new writer, or possibly do the revision him or herself. Outside of motion pictures, most of these scenarios are far less common.

We should mention that if the director is also the writer of the project, they must first sell the buyer on the material itself. This means either convincing them to read an original script or convincing them to hire the director to write an idea based on the pitch. In these cases, the pitch will be the same as a writer pitch – since what the director is actually selling at that stage is his or her writing. The listener will not be that interested in hearing directing ideas until they have read a screenplay they believe can be successful.

However, the bulk of the jobs for a director require them to pitch to get hired on someone else's project – in other words, an assignment. So, it should be no surprise that a director pitching an assignment has some overlap with aspects of a writer pitching an assignment, as we covered in an earlier chapter. The main differences in how a director will approach their pitch are based on what kind of project they are pitching.

The Director Pitch: Motion Picture.

Motion picture directors have a lot of responsibility. They are expected to be the primary artistic voice in the creation of the film. With Hollywood film production budgets routinely topping $100 million, the stakes are incredibly high. Even when the budget is modest, a qualified film director meeting for an open directing assignment is expected to pitch a seamless and detailed vision for all of the following facets (and more) of the production:

- The director's impression of the story – what works and doesn't work.
- The theme of the project, and how it relates to the director's *personal connection* to the material.
- Casting ideas – who they see in what roles.
- Visual style – how they will shoot the film, based on the content of the story and the expectations of the genre.
- Production design – the "look" of the film, including the integration of visual effects.
- Music, especially if it is important to the story.
- The plan to shoot and complete the production within the budget parameters and distribution time frame.

All of these elements will routinely be part of a director's pitch for an open feature film directing assignment. Because of the more comprehensive and visual nature of what the director is pitching, it's frequently the case that directors will bring some form of visual aid, such as a pitch book or sizzle reel, to help explain their approach. We will cover these aspects in more detail in the chapter on Props and Leave Behinds.

Of course, a director's pervious track record plays a role in how they pitch. If Martin Scorsese is pitching a crime drama, he gets the benefit of the doubt in many areas where another director has to prove him or herself. If you were pitching as a first or second time feature director, it would be wise to analyze your perceived strengths and weaknesses and tailor your pitch to address those areas. For example, if you are an established screenwriter wanting to direct your first project, the buyers will probably be comfortable with your grasp of story and character but may need greater evidence of your visual and technical abilities. On the other hand, if you've built a reputation directing music videos, the buyer probably already knows what you can do with imagery and editing, but they may be more concerned with your ability to bring in the emotional component of a feature. Try to anticipate the listener's concerns. Be sure to thoroughly address any area of weakness in your pitch preparations, while not ignoring your strengths.

One note: this pitching approach will be very similar for a director pitching an assignment in long-form television: television movies and mini-series.

The Director Pitch: Series Television.

Unlike directing motion pictures, where a director might work on the single film for one to three years, a director working in episodic television might work on a single episode for only one to five weeks. It's not unusual for an in-demand, freelance television director to direct five to ten episodes of *different* series over the course of a *single* year. We say freelance, because there are many series that have in-house producer/directors as part of the series staff. This is especially true for half-hour comedies. (For the sake of simplicity, we are excluding staff directors from this chapter.)

Because of their brief involvement with any particular series, freelance television directors have less influence over many of the elements in the episodes they direct. Series television is the domain of the series show-runner – the head writer, credited as executive producer. The show-runner has to make sure each episode fits into the flow of the on-going storylines, has consistency of characterization, tone, visual style, and is budgeted appropriately. They will be working on their series, worrying about these things, before and after a particular freelance director has come and gone.

As a result, most episodic directors pitch their ideas around the "margins." There is room for director creativity, but the ideas pitched are always judged in the context of what is important to the ongoing series. It will be part of the director's job to maintain the look and feel that has already been established. In fact, it is frequently the case that a director is hired *before* the episode they are to direct has even been written! This means there are usually two meetings, if the director has not previously directed for the series. The first meeting will be a general meeting about the series, often before the director is hired. And the second meeting will come after the director is handed the script they will shoot. (Of course, there are many meetings over the course of time the director works on an episode, but we are focusing here on the meetings where the director is selling himself or herself.)

The first meeting is usually held with the show-runner or the producer/director of the series, but only after the director has been "pre-approved" by the show-runner, network, and/or television studio. This pre-approval is based on things like the director's previous work history, their reel, and personal recommendations. The director's agenda for the first meeting typically includes:

- Demonstrating knowledge of the series, its storylines, characters and established visual style.
- Demonstrating the director is a reasonable person, collaborative, and can play well with others.
- The director asking questions about the series production schedule and problems on the series.
- The director's general assessment of the style of the series and what they might bring to their episode within the context of the established look and tone.

As director Arlene Sanford ("Grace and Frankie," "Nashville") puts it, "The first interview is much like a first date. And, like a first date, it is a chemistry check – do you both think you can get along with each other and the rest of the cast and crew and, if you are lucky, can you both have fun elevating the material and making the best show possible from the script at hand."

A second meeting is held after the writer has delivered a draft of the director's episode. (Of course, this will be the same meeting if a draft of the episode is available.) The agenda typically includes:

- The director discussing what the episode is really about and how it fits into the overall storylines of the series.
- The director identifying any story or logic problems with the script.
- The director identifying any production problems they envision, based on the draft.

Remember, television production schedules are grueling. Most series are looking for directors who will bring a clear personal vision and style to their episode but combined with fidelity to the series' existing artistic and budgetary parameters. The best director pitch will be the one that keeps both these priorities in balance.

As director Jeremy Podeswa ("Game of Thrones," "Boardwalk Empire") puts it, "Directing television is a balancing act, bringing your own vision to bear while at the same time serving the needs, tone, and established style of the particular show you're working on. When a director is hired, it's hoped they will elevate the show, while still working within the established vernacular. Nobody wants a director who goes rogue. You're expected to do your homework, play well with others, and make your days. These are all key."

The Director Pitch: Television Commercials.

As with a television series pitch, the world of commercial pitches is mostly dominated by established professionals, but not always. The proliferation of Internet content and cable channels means there are more opportunities than there once were. And whereas the predominant format for a television ad used to be 15 or 30 seconds, it's now common for many sponsors order ads intended for the Internet that might run one to three minutes, with shorter "cut downs" to run on television, social media, mobile, etc.

There are generally two kinds of pitches.

1) A director (and production company) trying to sell an idea/concept for a commercial directly to a sponsor, with no ad agency involved. This is the kind of ad a director might pitch to a local sponsor, possibly at the beginning of the director's career. The sponsor might be your local BBQ shack, florist, or other local retailer. In most cases, the production budgets are quite low, perhaps just a few thousand to a few tens of thousands of dollars. Some of these ads are produced and shot by the people who sell advertising air time on local TV as part of their service.

2) A director (and production company) pitching to get hired to direct and produce a commercial, based on a "script" (usually called a "board") that was crafted by an ad agency and approved by a sponsor. This is how the majority of ads are produced for sponsors that have regional, national or international brands. The production budgets can range from low six figures to over a million dollars, with the average perhaps in the $350,000 to $400,000 range. This does not include the cost to *air* the ad, which can range from $100,000 up to many millions of dollars to run an ad during the Super Bowl.

In some ways, the first kind of commercial pitch is analogous to an adaptation or rewrite pitch in that you're pitching an idea for *creating* the ad, but instead of being based on a pre-existing work like a book or script, you are pitching something based on a pre-existing product and/or brand. While there will be some creative leeway, fidelity *must* be paid to the existing brand/product and the current needs of the sponsor. Sponsors are very conservative with regards to the portrayal of their brand and products in commercials. One commercial director we spoke to joked that most sponsors would be just fine running 30 seconds of nothing but their logo.

The second kind of pitch is more restrictive because the director and production company are pitching to get a job based on a board that was probably the end result of 3 to 9 months of deliberations between a sponsor and the ad agency that crafted the script. A sponsor has a product they want to launch or promote, they hire an ad agency, the ad agency develops perhaps dozens of ideas, the sponsor whittles it down to one, the ad agency develops a script that goes through multiple revisions until the sponsor approves it. Finally, the script for the ad goes out for bids, and directors and production companies bid and pitch their approach to shooting the ad. In such a case, the board is essentially "locked" and the director is pitching his or her vision for how the script will be fully realized, from a production point of view. This second type of pitch has some similarities to episodic television, but replace the show-runner and network with the ad agency and sponsor, and condense the time allotted for pitching and production.

Award winning music video and commercial director Grady Hall explains, "Commercial pitches are highly competitive, creative battles that unfold in a matter of a couple of days. It's not unusual for a director to compete with two to five other directors who are just as experienced and as good as them, and sometimes with a 'name' feature director thrown into the mix. Anything less than a perfect, beautiful pitch of a brilliant and comprehensive vision will almost certainly lose. To have a chance at winning, you must come to understand the many layers of what the agency and sponsor want to convey in the ad, and then solve their communication problem in a way that both hooks viewers and delivers the message in a better way than they imagined."

Because scripts are locked in commercials, most director pitches involve the director's detailed and specific interpretations of the script within an *extremely* confined creative framework. However, there's still plenty of room for input around the edges and it's those aspects a director will pitch. Some of these aspects include:

- The director's personal connection to the concept and how that will impact the "feel" of the ad, and (more importantly) how they will connect that feeling to the *product*.
- The director's style, vision, and tone, and the way they will use these elements to grab the viewer's attention. What will be a visual effect? What will be live, animated, or both? What

innovative concepts and approaches does the director have in mind?
- The director's casting and performance ideas, assuming there are people in the ad.
- Design specifics, based on the locations suggested by the board.

Commercial directors think in *seconds* of screen time, so the specific choices they make for each of the above things needs to be precisely envisioned and conveyed.

If you want to pitch commercials, think of it like this: Every ad is trying to solve a problem. It could be any number of things – a sale, brand awareness, new product awareness, a change or update to a product, a product's competitive advantage, or an "image" issue – designed to create, reinforce or alter a specific brand identity in the minds of the consumer (for example, Exxon Mobil trying to promote its "green" credibility).

Of course, this "problem" is never a secret, and the sponsor or ad agency will surely let you know their needs. The ultimate goal of the director's pitch is to solve the problem in a way that elevates the ad, making it the best version of whatever the ad is trying to accomplish, all while staying within the budget parameters and the comfort zone of the sponsor.

Sample Commercial Pitch.

Below is a sample outline for a pitch that a commercial director might use to get hired, based on an existing board that was put out for bids. This is the second kind of pitch we described above and the most common type in the commercial world. Remember, while the board in this sample is "locked," there's always room for creative interpretation and enhancement, and articulating these things is the essence of the pitch. In the real world, a director's pitch would be done in tandem with a presentation of budget and other production matters. Also, the pitch would surely incorporate the *significant* use of a treatment – visual aids, created by the director, and his or her team, to help the agency and sponsor understand the director's *specific* vision. Of course, the creation of budgets and treatments and reels are beyond the scope of this book.

Let's imagine you are a director who was sent the board for AT&T voice services – what they used to call a "landline." The client wants a 30-second ad with a couple of 15-second cut downs. You're receiving this board (informally called "the creative") because the ad agency producer liked your previous work and is considering you for the job, along with three or four other top directors. There would likely be an initial call where the various agency creatives walk you through the board. This initial conversation is your opportunity to listen and ask questions, but the agency will still expect you to bring a strong point of view. Prior to this call, you should have developed your approach and researched other recent ads that the sponsor has ordered. This initial call is your chance to fill in some of the gaps in your knowledge and fine-tune your approach. By the end of the call, you should have all the information you need to fully develop your official pitch.

So, let's assume the call went well, and you've been invited back to deliver your complete presentation. Below is an outline for the pitch. Remember, this is just an outline. An actual pitch would go into much greater detail and continue to develop the vision the director is presenting.

The ad portrays a woman ("Anne") who is packing some things and finds her old personal phone book. In her little book, she sees the name "Nicole" and a "home" phone number written in faded pencil. On a whim, she decides to call it. She is amazed and pleased to discover that the old home number is still active, and her old college roommate answers, allowing the college friends to reconnect. The college roommate explains that an AT&T voice service number can "travel" with her, wherever she goes. The tagline will be, "AT&T. Friendship is timeless."

The first thing the ad agency will want to hear is the director's initial response to the ad. This is equivalent to the personal connection we've discussed in this book, so make it personal.

The ad reminds me of when I was a child growing up in the country. Our home was very isolated and our landline was our only immediate connection to the outside world. Yes, we now all have the Internet and texting, but we forget how "cold" those devices can be, and people change their cell phone numbers over the years, so it's easy to lose touch. There's nothing like the feeling you get when you know you can pick up the phone, call a number, and hear someone's voice – a parent, loved one, or old friend...

Next, identify what you think the ad is really "about" as it relates to the product and brand. It is <u>very important</u> to identify the essence of the ad, because you are about to describe your unique vision to bring this concept to life in the best possible way. However, do not belabor and regurgitate what the ad agency already knows.

Digging into the creative, it really struck me how easy it is for friends to become disconnected in our supposedly "connected" world, and how a simple thing, like an enduring landline, can bring them back together...

...It's one of those occasions where, yes, we're selling a service, but its real power is how it connects people on a personal level... reminding viewers of a simple human joy that everyone can relate to, and how AT&T technology, engineering, and service is all about delivering something on a very personal level for the characters in the ad, and the consumer...

Now expand on this and talk about the message, tone or "feeling" the ad should convey. Explain how this quality amplifies or enhances the existing brand. What does it say about the core nature of the brand or product? How will it appeal to its intended market?

I want to make sure we get an emotional tug in this ad. AT&T voice service is not just an 'appliance' – it's a bond and <u>lifeline</u> that reconnects two old friends in profound ways...

Now explain your specific approach to the ad. This is the most important part of your pitch, and it's what the sponsor will be most interested to hear. Despite a locked script, there are invariably many decisions that will need to be made to realize your vision based on what's in the board. These choices/decisions might include: casting, cinematography, setting, music, locations, animation, effects, production design, color palette, etc. Make sure you justify your choices, based on the themes and purposes you've just established.

I would start by casting two very different-looking actors in their mid-30s. I want to do everything I can to quickly imply why the characters might have drifted apart. They should clearly be from different walks of life. Perhaps they met in college when they were randomly paired as freshman roommates. They became close friends. But after graduation, they returned to their very different worlds and lost contact with each other. They should be mid-30s because this is long enough for the characters to have really lost touch and also makes them old enough to remember the days before things like Facebook, before everyone had a cell phone...

Notice how the pitch stays focused on a central theme, never strays much, and makes each point simple and easy to follow. The goal is to be impressive and to the point, but not so bold as to stray outside the bounds of the locked board that took the agency perhaps six months to get approved! If you pitch a significant change to the board, the agency will have run the proposed changes back to their creative executives, and then reopen the debate with the client (the sponsor). No one's going to do this. More likely, you just won't get the job.

Let's continue.

Films and TV series have the luxury of setting up great moments like this with 30 minutes of context, but we need to achieve the same emotional connection in seconds – and that's why my approach would be to make sure every detail and piece of "film grammar" is unified – almost like a period piece, but where the period is "now," creating deeper characters, backstories, and casting actors who could absolutely pull off the film version of this – even if some of those details don't end up on screen. It's this added depth and feature narrative approach that will bring it to life. We want viewers to walk in the shoes of our characters and project their own lives into the narrative...

...I also want to set up a contrast between the lives of the characters in the use of setting and production design. I want to make it clear that Anne represents a more transient life, while Nicole is all about stability. When we meet Anne, she's packing up things in her apartment, probably moving yet again. Maybe she just broke up with a boyfriend. She's lonely. She's surrounded by boxes. She's in a cramped closet, and this is where she finds here old personal phone book. Nicole, by contrast, answers her phone in the spacious kitchen of her brightly lit home. Everything about Nicole's kitchen says permanence, like something out of the Restoration Hardware catalog...

...The lighting and color palette will also contrast. Anne's apartment will be muted yellows and reds, whereas Nicole's kitchen will be whites and pastels – brightly lit and airy. But as the conversation develops, Anne will walk out of closet and towards a picture window in her living room – also light and airy. Subtly, as the two characters reconnect, the look of Anne's world will become more like Nicole's, visually connecting the two lives in the minds of the viewer...

And so on.

Do you see how all the director's specific choices are all designed to take the core of what's already in the board and amplify it? Nothing is extraneous. The director is essentially re-pitching the *same* ad *back* to the agency and sponsor in a way that is fully realized and will bring out the best version of the ad.

PITCHING STYLE AND PRESENTATION

Almost everything we've discussed so far has to do with the nuts and bolts of crafting a pitch. For the rest of the book we will talk about elements of personal style, presentation and etiquette. For some people, much of this will come naturally. However, if you've never been to a Hollywood meeting, some of the conventions and customs may seem strange. And it's difficult to know what you don't know. So, if some of what we tell you seems obvious, bear with us. Our goal is to give you an understanding of what to expect and what is expected of you so that you'll be more comfortable.

Respect.

A pitch is a social interaction between two parties, the goal of which involves conveying an artistic experience from one person to another. And as a social interaction, it shares many of the same qualities as other kinds of social interactions. There are aspects of trust, confidence, authority, respect, presentation and style all mixed in together.

Think about the person you're pitching to. Put yourself in their shoes. Whether they are your agent, your friend, a producer, or a buyer, don't assume that what's in your head is what you're communicating. If they don't grasp your genius, give them a break. First of all, if they're on the buyer side of the desk, they're probably hearing a lot of pitches during the course of a month. Their goal is to find the one or two that will be right for their company. And they are doing it while attempting to balance the other responsibilities of their job.

If you're pitching to a creative executive, it's likely that they may have to convince their boss and maybe a studio exec that your pitch is a winner. They may have to re-pitch your idea without you there. And their job depends on a fair level of success when they do this. Remember, if they do buy your pitch, they are probably going to spend years of their life working on the project, so they better like it an awful lot.

A pitch is a sales tool, but it's not a con job. If you're in this for the long haul, the goal is to find the right home for your story, not trick someone into writing you a check. Let your story be what it wants to be. If you're pitching to the right buyer, then they'll see it. If they don't, either you didn't convey your idea properly, or they weren't the right buyer.

So, do your listener a favor; be respectful of the hard work they do.

A few other tips about consideration for your listener:

- Learn to be a good listener. Above and beyond its own intrinsic value, being a good listener will help you craft your pitch and tailor it to the buyer's needs.
- Know the person you're pitching to. Never go into a pitch without knowing a little about the background of the recipient, their other projects, and what their job is. Part of your job when you meet is to connect with the other person. Getting to know them is the first step and may lead to a long-term association, whether you sell this one pitch or not.
- Know your subject. We've covered this before. It's not enough to just know your pitch. Become an expert on the various facets of your topic. If your pitch goes well, the buyer

will ask questions. Meeting those questions unprepared is an amateur mistake.
- Take "no" for an answer. If you get resistance to your ideas, the worst thing you can do is argue. People who listen to pitches do it for a living, and they know what they like and don't like. If they didn't respond to your initial presentation, you will not be able to argue them into liking your story. Yes, we've all heard tales of successful people who say "I never take no for an answer." What they don't tell you is that the "yes" can take years to get. Take no for an answer and live to fight another day.
- Speak clearly. It is good to be enthusiastic, but don't speak so quickly the listener will have difficulty keeping up. If you have an accent (or if English is not your primary language), work on minimizing it and speak even more slowly.
- Try to get the contact information of the people you meet when you pitch. Send them a thank you e-mail or note after the meeting. You can't force them to reply, but if they do, that's great. Next time you have a project, you might be able to contact the buyer directly, which is beneficial. Long-term careers are based on personal relationships in Hollywood.

Confidence.

Again, put yourself in the buyer's shoes. You are asking them to risk their company's money on you and your idea. And if you don't seem confident in your abilities and your project, then they will not want to take that risk.

Let's say you are interviewing two contractors to remodel your kitchen. The first has an easygoing manner as he clearly lays out his ideas for the remodel, casually dropping the occasional technical term into his presentation. When you ask him questions, he's able to answer them and explain why he thinks his approach is the best. You get the impression he's done it a thousand times before.

The second seems nervous and is constantly referring to notes as he lays out his ideas. At one point he gets confused, and when you ask him about a suggestion he's made, he can't really explain the reasons behind it. He apologizes for his anxiety, saying this is only the third kitchen remodel he's bid on.

Which do you hire?

It's hard to just "be confident," but two things can help. First, don't think about the pitch as a job interview. Think about it as an opportunity for your listener to get involved in a project you love, should they also love it. Take the attitude that someone will buy this pitch – maybe it will be this person, but if not, it'll probably be the next. Consider it to be as much their opportunity as yours, but remember that arrogance and confidence are not the same thing.

Second, don't pitch an idea if you're not confident about it. Seriously, you must have an idea that you think would make a great movie or television show, right? If not, why are you in this business? If you pitch an idea you genuinely think is great then you have a much better chance of pitching it with confidence. Similarly, work out all the beats of the idea even if you don't pitch them all. If your story is half-baked, it will show.

It is helpful if you can get everyone in the room comfortable, and that takes an air of confidence. If you're anxious and desperate it will make the buyer uncomfortable. This is also why telling how you got the inspiration for the story is a great way to open. It's a natural way to ease into your story.

Confidence is even more critical for directors and producers. You are asking the listener to place their trust in you to manage a production and supervise perhaps hundreds of people. The person considering your pitch wants someone who exudes authority – without being a jerk. That last part is also critical. The executive will have to work even more closely with the producer and director of the project than the writer. They want it to be a reasonably pleasant experience.

To Memorize or Not to Memorize.

Hopefully, you have your log line down pat, along with the core elements like title, tone/rating/genre, and personal connection. You should be able to summon these things at will, whether you're doing a scheduled pitch or one on the fly. But longer pitches usually require a strategy for recalling vastly more information, usually related to plot.

Some writers can memorize their pitch word-for-word and then perform it like an actor. If you are a good actor, this might work for you, but there are some risks and problems with this approach. First of all, it can give you stage fright. You put a lot of pressure on yourself to do things a certain way, and if/when something goes wrong it can derail you. Second, it makes it harder to adapt to a changing situation. Your listener might interrupt you with questions. Or, what if you sense they are getting bored? What if the listener asks you to do a shorter version than you've memorized because they have another meeting in five minutes? These are all examples of things that can throw you if you are locked into a presentation through rote memorization. In any case, most writers are not savants and are not able to memorize fifteen minutes of story. Most will bring written notes.

Bringing detailed, written notes to a pitch meeting is perfectly acceptable and is really the norm. The people you are pitching to understand the challenges you face when telling a story, and, by and large, they want you to succeed.

So, what kind of written notes should you bring? It depends on what you think you will need. We've seen writers who bring a few index cards and we've seen writers who bring twenty pages of text. There are some other considerations with this decision that are unrelated to your story. We will get into them shortly.

The one thing to avoid is reading your notes verbatim. It can come off as tedious and annoying.

We suggest you create a bullet-point outline for your pitch, then improvise based on that outline. Even though you're going to improvise, you'll want to rehearse many times, often with other people, until you know it backwards and forwards. Things that get a good response in your rehearsals will lodge in your mind from positive reinforcement, and you'll naturally deliver them that way in the meeting, but you won't feel pressured to get it exactly right. Your pitches will become more casual and conversational.

```
The Heist                           Card 3
- John levels with Tony, loans tough to get, when...
- GUNSHOTS fired!
- THREE ARMED/MASKED MEN storm the bank!
- Order everyone to get on floor. All do so, but...
- Not John, who stays with helpless Tony.
- BANK GUARD makes his move and...
- Guard is quickly disarmed. BUT NOT OF LEG HOLSTER!
- John SEES this, but what can he do? He's no hero!
```

In the meeting, you can hold a page or two with the bullet points or bring index cards. As we've said, it won't raise any eyebrows if you work from notes. However, you should have rehearsed so much that you barely have to refer to the notes. You want to engage the listener with eye contact, not stare at your notes. Your notes are a safety net, just in case you lose your train of thought.

Rehearsal is critical. You will be nervous when you pitch. Most people are. You also have to be prepared for bizarre interruptions and distractions. So, the more you've rehearsed, the better you'll be able to handle the stress of the room. You can rehearse into the mirror, or to your teddy bear, or to a spot on the wall; but you should do at least a few pitches to actual people. It enables you to gauge their response to various things, and you can find out where they get confused or misinterpret something. Rehearsing is the single greatest thing you can do to improve your pitching. As writer/director Eric Heisserer ("Arrival," "Lights Out") says, "Like everything, repetition and practice has made it bearable. You improve by doing something over and over. And if you're looking to make screenwriting a career, you have to accept that you'll work up a hundred pitches (or more) in your tenure."

Like it or not, a pitch is a performance. And most writers don't like it. You don't have to master the art of song and dance to pitch, but there are a few skills you may need to develop.

First, pitch with energy and enthusiasm. Think about it – if you don't like your story, why should your listener? If you slump back, mumbling in a monotone while you pick at a loose thread on your jeans, they are going to think that your pitch bores even you. This doesn't mean you have to jump around and act out the story. Try to harness the kind of energy and attitude you have when describing a great movie to a friend.

Second, tell your story in straightforward, declarative sentences. Consider the following example of a pitch, as it might be delivered verbally:

"So, it's about this archeologist, right? And he's kind of adventurous. He runs around with, you know, a bullwhip? And he's sort of, like, this expert with it. So, the FBI comes to him because they're a little suspicious of this other archeologist who they kind of think could be, like, friendly to the Nazis or something."

When you speak your sentences in a questioning way, you seem unsure of your story. Is he an archeologist or not? If you don't know, who does? Also, you want to avoid weak phrases: sort of, kind of, a little, like, a bit. It's natural to use these in speech, but it weakens the drama of your story in a pitch. As you rehearse, make an effort to eliminate these kinds of words and phrases.

Many times, we're unaware we're speaking this way, so it might help to videotape yourself when you practice your pitch.

Look at the same paragraph above re-formed with direct, declarative sentences:

"It's about an adventurous archeologist, a man's man, who's an expert with a bullwhip. The FBI comes to him because they're suspicious that another archeologist – an old friend – might be in league with the Nazis."

Much better, right?

The truth is, a relaxed and confident writer makes every pitch stronger. But that's probably an impossible goal. You will be nervous. So, manage it by being prepared. Learning to deliver a good pitch is an ongoing process. So just keep rehearsing and you will get better at it.

One last bit of advice: modulate your performance based on the content of your story. Far too often we've seen beginning filmmakers pitch their stories as if every beat had the same dramatic weight. Don't pitch, "John spends the morning filling out bank forms" in the same way you'd pitch, "John looks up – a guy wearing a ski mask is pointing a chrome .357 Magnum in his face!" If you come to a dramatic moment in your story, pitch it dramatically! If you come to an exciting action moment in your story, you may want to quicken the pacing of your pitch.

Don't Look for Approval, Just Tell Your Story.

This is related to being confident. Seeking approval from the listener in your tone and style is a mistake. Pitching is not like a conversation where the talker waits for the listener to respond before continuing. It is disconcerting and distracting for the buyer if they feel they have to encourage you that you are doing well. The listener expects a committed point of view. Give it to them. Unfortunately, it sometimes happens that the person(s) listening to your pitch is truly unresponsive – they just sit there, impassive and stone-faced, like a Sphinx. When this happens, it's known as a "cold room."

Writer/Director John Gray ("Ghost Whisperer," "White Irish Drinkers") has sold many pitches and has a strategy for dealing with these situations. Says Gray, "I've had a fair amount of luck selling pitches over the years, and when I'm in a room, I try to make it fun for me and for the buyer. However, you have to learn to keep your energy and passion in high gear even when faced with a 'cold room.' If I feel the buyer is not paying attention, is bored with life in general, or (as once happened to me) they keep looking over my shoulder at the TV that's playing behind me, I like to glance occasionally at my producing partner(s) and draw some positive energy from them. My attitude is always, 'I'm going to pitch this as if these people can't wait to hear my next word.' I'm going to make this my best pitch."

Getting Questions and Handling Interruptions.

It's not unusual to get questions from your listener. Sometimes they will occur during your pitch, especially if you are confusing or don't speak clearly. However, if you've rehearsed properly, this should be minimal. The listener might even offer up ideas or suggestions for changes to your story as you tell it. While you might find this a little annoying, it means your listener is engaged with your pitch. Embrace it. This doesn't mean you have to agree and say "yes" right in that moment. If the listener is asking for a big change, you might want to ask the listener if you can discuss it after the pitch. If the answer to the question is an easy yes, say "yes." If the answer is emphatically no, once again, ask to discuss it after the pitch is over. What you want to avoid is getting into a debate while you are in the flow of your story.

When your pitch is over, you may get some comments and questions about it. With rewrite or director pitches, sometimes the listener will want to discuss each point or suggestion as you make it, turning the pitch into more of a conversation. How you handle comments and questions is every bit as important as the presentation itself.

The number one rule is don't get defensive. Your reaction to questions and comments will affect how the buyer will remember you. If you get angry or argumentative, they are going to think of you as someone who is difficult to work with.

Few story ideas are completely without some commercial liability, and don't be surprised if this is the first thing the buyer mentions. Be careful not to step outside your expertise. For example, if they ask you what you think the budget would be, you should not venture a hard number unless you're a line producer. (The exception is if you're making a presentation of your completed script to a financier for an independent film, in which case you better have a detailed budget created by an experienced line producer.) Try to analyze where the listener's question is coming from. Are they worried it's going to be too expensive? You might use the question as an opportunity to describe how you're going to approach the story in a way that keeps costs down. (Note that some genres are supposed to be expensive. For example, if you're pitching an epic, science fiction film, it ought to have spectacle.)

When a buyer has comments, the first thing you should do is listen. Occasionally, writers will be so caught up in the intensity of the situation that they'll jump in before the other person has even finished speaking. Sometimes the writer's response can even be unrelated to the buyer's concern. So listen to what the buyer is saying and take a moment to think about it.

This is particularly tough to do when the buyer criticizes something about your pitch. Your natural instinct is to defend yourself. But pay attention to what they are really saying. If you think there is relevant information that might clarify something they missed, share it. If you have an idea of how to solve a specific problem, suggest it. However, if they really just didn't respond to your characters, you are probably not going to change their mind.

On the bright side, their criticism may help you shape the story into something more viable. Usually, you're going to pitch the same idea many times. Producers and executives in this industry, despite their reputation, are mostly smart and savvy people when it comes to story. Keep in mind, you may have written three scripts, but they may have developed 100. If someone makes a suggestion for your story, it's worth considering whether to incorporate it before the next pitch.

However, you should not automatically assume every bit of feedback you get is right. A comment might be based on a misunderstanding or an element of personal taste not shared by the average listener. Sometimes smart people just say stupid things. But do give it some consideration. Maybe they have a point, and sometimes you will get feedback that you won't initially recognize as a solution to something. Regardless, if you hear the same criticism repeatedly, you better address it before the next time you pitch the project.

One question you might encounter is, "If we don't buy this pitch, will you spec it?" The worst answer is "no." You've just told them you don't really believe in your project. And if you don't, why should they?

But if you say "yes," they'll probably smile and say, "Great, send it to us when it's done." This isn't all bad – you've got someone who will read the script, someday. The downside is that you've also just agreed to work for free and killed any chance of selling it as a pitch.

We suggest you respond with something like, "I love this idea and I'm definitely going to write it, but my agent is setting up a bunch of meetings, so I hope someone will see the potential in it that I do." This is a not-so-subtle threat that if they don't step up, they might miss out. Of course, this often won't work!

HOW A MEETING WORKS

It's useful to have some idea of what's going to happen when you go into a meeting. If nothing else, it might help you to relax a little. And, truth be told, even experienced screenwriters tend to spend an inordinate amount of time discussing this kind of thing.

General Meetings.

One of the most common types of meeting you'll have if you are a writer or director is what is known as a "general meeting." You get a general meeting when someone has read some of your work or maybe seen one of your films (if you are a director) and wants to meet you. The majority of the time you will be meeting with one person, but there could be two, three, or even more. There might be more than one producer or development exec at the company who wants to meet you, and/or there might be an intern or assistant to take notes. Most general meetings will be with producers or the people who work for producers, sometimes called creative executives or development executives. Needless to say, you should know the job title of everyone you will be meeting in advance. If someone is a senior vice-president and you call him or her a "development executive," they might be insulted. Most people work hard for their titles. Know whom you are addressing.

"LIAR LIAR"
by Paul Guay

On March 18, 1990, I jotted down an idea for a movie: "For one day, a guy who's been a liar must tell the truth."

On March 18, 1997, my then-writing partner and I attended the world premiere of "Liar, Liar."

What happened in the intervening seven years?

First, we turned my idea into a pitch. In 1990 we pitched a basic story to nine different companies.

All of them turned it down.

One company said they already had two liar projects in development. Another thought it might be interesting if our hero were four years old. We agreed it might be interesting. Stupid, but interesting. (We may not have said that aloud.)

We moved on to other projects, including "The Little Rascals," when on April 14, 1994, we had a general meeting at Imagine with David Friendly. I didn't particularly want to go, because in my experience, general meetings – meetings where you're not discussing one of your specific projects or one of their specific projects – were a waste of time. But I went.

How a Meeting Works

David mentions that Brian Grazer has an idea for a film about a liar.

Being young and full of ourselves, we say, "Stop!" And before David can tell us Brian's idea, we tell him ours.

David says, "That's very interesting. Unfortunately, Brian's not in the office right now. When he gets back, I'll tell him your idea."

At this point, we've been to a lot of meetings. We know when we're being given a handjob. We think, "Yeah, that's gonna happen."

We're in the lobby getting our parking validated, which is the highpoint of the day for us, when a force of nature speeds by at 200 mph with spiky hair. This, of course, is Brian. Through the glass door, we see him confer with David.

Then Brian opens the door and sticks his head out. "You guys have a minute?"

We figure what the hell, we're here already, we've validated our parking, it's the president of Imagine – sure, we can spare a minute.

We go into Brian's office and sit. "So tell me about your idea."

"Well, it's about a guy who's a liar –"

Brian pounds his desk twice. "I love it! I love it! What does he do?"

"Well, we think he's a lawyer –"

Brian pounds his desk twice more. "A lawyer who's a liar! I love it! We're gonna make this movie."

My partner and I walk out of there asking, "What the hell just happened?"

We leave Imagine's offices in Century City. By the time we get to my house in Santa Monica, our agent is on the phone, telling us we have a deal.

What do we learn from this, boys and girls?

One thing we learn is: Don't blow off meetings. You never know when you might meet the right person at the right time.

For whatever reason – maybe because he too had an idea for a film about a liar (which we never got around to hearing), maybe because at that moment he wasn't particularly a fan of lawyers – Brian Grazer was the right person at the right time. While we had a lot more than two sentences to offer, Brian saw a movie in our two sentences.

I'm glad we decided to go to the meeting.

Now all we had to do was write the damn thing.

Etiquette.

Get there on time – and then be prepared to wait. Yes, people in Hollywood are busy, but sometimes there's a bit of a power play that happens. They get to keep you waiting to prove they're more powerful than you. The wait is actually good. It gives you a chance to settle in and get your bearings. And, if you've just had to walk halfway across the studio lot on a hot September day, it gives you a chance to cool down.

Bring a notebook and something to write with. You are a professional going into a business meeting – be prepared. If the buyer gives you feedback on your pitch, write it down. This serves two purposes. First of all, you'll remember everything more clearly. Second, it will allow you to digest what has been said before responding. It's not uncommon for writers to have knee-jerk negative reactions to suggestions. If you give yourself time to consider the comments, you may discover merit that wasn't immediately obvious. And even if the suggestion is off base, you don't want to get in a heated argument with the buyer.

Before you start the meeting, the assistant or receptionist will ask if you'd like anything to drink. We recommend water, even if you're not thirsty. You may get dry mouth during the meeting, plus it gives you a prop. If you need a few seconds to think over how to answer a question, you can take a drink to buy some time. Don't ask for soda – it will make you burp. Avoid coffee or tea. They may not cool down enough to drink before the end of the meeting, and if you're nervous, caffeine might exacerbate the problem.

We know this stuff seems silly. But sometimes little things like this can make the difference between a good meeting and a bad one. At the very least, they can affect your comfort level.

Typically, you'll meet in the producer or exec's office. Other times you'll meet in a conference room. Much more rarely (assuming you're dealing with established professionals), you might meet in a coffee shop, restaurant, hotel bar, or some other venue. If the meeting is in an office, they most likely will have a seating area. They'll come out from behind the desk and meet with you in that more casual setting.

In the Room.

If you're meeting in the buyer's office, the seating areas will usually have a couch. A really *soft, comfy* couch. Try not to sit on it. You will sink back into it and it will sap your energy. If you do end up on the couch, sit forward on the edge. If there are multiple people in the meeting, pick a spot where you can look at all of them with relatively little head movement. You don't want to be swiveling your head back and forth like you're at a tennis match.

If you happen to get a lunch or coffee meeting, which is rare when starting out, first-date rules apply: Don't order anything too messy or hard to eat. It'll distract you, and the risk of an embarrassing incident is high. Don't arrive too hungry, either. This is about business, not about eating. On the plus side, the writer never pays in these situations.

The meeting will probably last about thirty minutes. It will start with some small talk. They'll probably ask where you're from and how you got started in the business. They may discuss the script of yours that they read (if you're a writer) or your sample reel or film (if you're a director). Your goal here is to be charming and pleasant – the kind of person they'd like to work with. It's also good to convey an interesting life story. It implies you'll have an interesting point of view in your work. You might want to consider, in advance, what's interesting about your life story, so you can make sure to work it into this conversation. At some point, they'll probably say something like, "So, what else are you working on now?" It is critical that you have an answer to this question. The perception of activity is important. Just don't be a braggart. Talk about the other project you are researching or lining up to write or pitch. If the buyer hears something that piques their interest, they may ask you to elaborate.

Although technically this is a get-to-know-you meeting, it's likely you will be pitching your next idea. If so, the pitch should be fairly casual and not too long. This is a perfect opportunity to wield the 5-minute version of your idea. They probably aren't buying… but they might. Mostly you're trying to let them know you have other good ideas and getting them excited to read your next spec when it's done. You never know… if the pitch is good enough, you might just sell it in the room.

One Meeting, One Idea.

We recommend that you don't pitch more than a single idea in most situations. It shows that you are committed and passionate about that idea, not just throwing ideas out to see what sticks. But it's also advisable to have a "doorknob pitch" ready if they don't respond to the first one. A doorknob pitch is a brief (usually two minutes or less) pitch of a rough idea. It's called a doorknob pitch because of the image that you would deliver it as your hand is on the doorknob on your way out, kind of an, "Oh, I almost forgot" attitude. Of course, you don't actually do it that way. It comes at the tail end of the meeting and is done in a quick, off-the-cuff manner. You can preface it by saying something like, "This isn't fully developed, but there is another idea I've been kicking around." If they like it, you can ask to come back and give them the full pitch in a week or two after you've "had time to work it all out." The spec pilot for "Mad Men" was probably the most famous doorknob pitch in TV history. Weiner had sent his old spec pilot for "Mad Men" to AMC as a writing sample to pitch an entirely different series. But when AMC passed on the pitch, Weiner pitched the series based on his spec. The rest is history.

It's also possible someone will pitch you an idea in the general meeting. It might be an idea of the producer's, a newspaper article, maybe even someone else's script. "We want to do something set during Spring Break," to use our previous example. Great, right? But there's a good news/bad news aspect to this. On the one hand, if they are pitching you an idea, presumably that means they like it. This is a leg-up over coming in "cold" and just hoping you will have an idea someone else will like. On the other hand, many of the ideas that might come to you this way will be highly unformed, and sometimes it is just a way to get some "free" feedback. So, if this happens, take it seriously, but with a grain of salt. You probably don't want to go off and come back with twenty pages of notes based on the idea you were handed. It would be a better use of your time to think in broad strokes about how you'd approach the subject, and relay that back to the source.

If you are pitched something in this manner, attempt to get some background and find out why they are pitching it to you. Some questions you might ask, where applicable: "Do you control the rights?" "How long have you been interested in this idea?" "Is this set up somewhere?" If not, "Who do you think might buy something like this?"

The answers to these questions can help you understand how real the project is, and how much of your time it's worth. Many projects originate this way, but it can also be a huge waste of your time if you're not smart about it. Your decision will depend on where you are in your career and what other options you might have at the time. You might also consider who is asking you to do this work. Are they someone who can commission you to write a script if you present a great take on the idea? Are they someone you're eager to work with? Even if the project is unlikely to come to fruition, exploring the project with the buyer or producer can help build the relationship with them and show them how you work.

Pitch Meetings.

General meetings are usually with people whom you haven't met previously. If things go well, you can go back again someday and pitch other ideas. Those later meetings are similar, except the get-to-know you part is truncated (since they already know you). In these cases, you would be expected to deliver a fully developed pitch – 10 to 15 minutes.

These types of meetings end somewhat differently. When the pitch is over, the buyer will most likely not tell you how they feel. They probably have to discuss it with other people in the office before they can buy it. Or, they may know it's not a project for them and just tell you that right up front. However, the vast majority of passes happen somewhere between a day and a week later, and usually come to you via your producer or agent. If they have criticisms at the end of the meeting, you have to be careful how you respond. Try to determine if they are asking questions and genuinely want answers, or if they are just justifying the coming pass. If the latter, you should listen politely, but there's no point in getting into a detailed discussion of their issues. Frequently, the response to your pitch can be misleading. Nobody likes to deliver bad news, so the listener may be very encouraging yet have no intention of buying your story. Be careful not to overreact to a positive, but vague, response.

Wrapping it Up.

After the meeting, say goodbye and leave. Whatever happens, don't get too stressed out. There will be other meetings in your future.

If, prior to meeting with buyers, a producer has decided they like your pitch, you will most likely collaborate and hone it with them. It is not at all unusual to come back and re-do a revised version of the pitch several times over a period of months until the producer is happy with it. The next step is to take it to a studio. Now the producer will be going with you to the meeting. They will help set you up to tell your story and help keep things running smoothly. They will let you do the actual pitching – you're the one the studio exec wants to hear – though the producer may jump in with a quick reminder if you forget something.

There are variations on this process. The producer may have you pitch to a star or director who is looking for a project before going to the studio. If the star or director attaches himself or herself to the project, they may then join you in the studio pitch. Or they may not. It is also not uncommon to have to pitch your way up through the ranks of the studio. This is why we said earlier that selling a pitch is not always easier or less time consuming than writing a spec script.

HOW TO BEHAVE IN A MEETING

Looking Professional.

Part of presentation is how you look. A pitch is a business meeting – in a sense it's a job interview – so you should dress appropriately and pay attention to basic hygiene. Of course, what's appropriate attire in Hollywood can be different from what's appropriate in other industries.

You don't have to wear a business suit. In fact, in most Hollywood creative meetings that would be very unusual. You are supposed to be the creative talent – they don't want you to look like a lawyer. However, you also don't want to look like the guy who washes the cars in the valet parking.

Wear something casual but nice, something that makes you feel comfortable and good about yourself.

Acting Professional.

Ask any professional writer or director about pitching, and before long you will undoubtedly be hearing horror stories about interruptions or rudeness from the listener. We can't possibly begin to cover all of the possible interruptions and distractions you may face. But we can give you some general guidelines that should apply in most situations.

The number-one rule is "Never lose your cool." Everyone can have a bad day. Whatever happens, smile and be gracious – even if they aren't. When you pitch, of course you're trying to sell that idea. More importantly, you're starting/building/maintaining your relationship with the listener. If they're not interested in this pitch, you want the opportunity to come back with the next one. So, don't get angry or frustrated... or, if you do, don't let it show.

The most common type of disruption you'll encounter is your listener taking a phone call. Our advice is simply to stop pitching, wait quietly, and when they're done just pick up where you left off as if nothing had happened. This works for most types of interruptions.

On other occasions, someone may join the pitch late – another exec or producer you didn't know was going to be there. If they are not an assistant or intern, quickly catch them up on the story by giving the log line, character information and critical plot beats, but avoid going into great detail so you don't bore the person or people who were there from the start.

Some buyers will sit quietly and listen to your pitch in its entirety. Others will interrupt and ask questions. Some will make suggestions. As we said before, don't let this throw you. Answer their questions and try to address their suggestions with a grateful attitude. Whatever you do, don't criticize their ideas! They don't like criticism any more than you do, and they're not the one in the room trying to sell something!

When you're just starting out, every pitch can feel like it's a make-or-break situation for your career. Trust us, it's not. You'll get other opportunities. So, if things don't go perfectly, don't overreact.

PROPS AND LEAVE-BEHINDS

Props.

> In a formal pitch meeting, it's sometimes useful to bring supplemental materials to help sell the project, story, or ideas being presented. These supplemental materials are collectively referred to as "props." While some business presentations will regularly use things like graphics with pie charts and PowerPoint presentations, these kinds of things are rarely used in the entertainment industry – at least for the creative side of showbiz. Instead, writers, directors and producers in Hollywood will occasionally use things like concept art, photos, storyboards, and short videos ("sizzle reels") to help convey their ideas.
>
> In recent years, we've noticed many film schools have emphasized the importance of teaching their students how to create some of these elements. However, we have a more nuanced point of view about the value of props. First, many pitches are not part of a formal meeting, but rather take place in a more casual setting, are spontaneous, or sometimes by phone, meaning you may not have or be able to use props. What then? Furthermore, bringing out a prop in a general meeting can seem a little weird or desperate – a general meeting is ostensibly a more casual conversation. Finally, the use of props can be an asset in a formal pitch, but not always. Let's examine this last point in more detail.

It used to be that, for writers, bringing visual aids or props into a pitch to help sell a story was considered goofy and amateurish. These days, things have changed – somewhat. Some writers now bring concept art, and maybe even a sizzle reel or short video to some pitch meetings. (Emphasize *short* – two to five minutes at most if you're going to show it in the meeting.) For directors and producers, it has always been more customary to bring props to a pitch, based on the nature of those jobs as compared to writers, whose job is primarily telling stories.

If you are a writer in a formal pitch setting, the majority of the time you should rely purely on your storytelling ability to sell your pitch. You are there to paint a picture with words, and that's what most buyers will expect. In most cases, that's all they will need. For example, if you're pitching something like a romantic comedy, don't bring a wedding cake to the pitch. It will seem gimmicky and maybe even annoying to a busy buyer, who just wants to hear the pitch and move on to their next appointment.

A good rule of thumb is that if a visual aid or prop helps make something clearer for the listener related to the story, you may wish to bring it. If the prop is organic to the concept, it can help, but if not, there's a risk it will smack of "trying too hard." In general, try to steer away from bringing "marketing materials." No one expects you to bring a one-sheet if there's no script yet. If you're pitching with a producer in the room, you might want to let them handle the props part of the pitch. Regarding props for a writer, our rule of thumbs is, "when in doubt, leave it out."

So, when is bringing a prop a good idea? If your story is based on underlying material – a comic book or a novel, for example – bring a copy with you and drop it on the coffee table before you pitch. It helps the project feel more substantial. Other useful props are those that help illustrate your story. If you were pitching a movie about, say, an actual elite military unit and you had some photos or video of that unit in action, it would be helpful to make them part of the presentation. Or if you were pitching a true story or some other unfamiliar topic where the buyer's ability to visualize the subject matter is key, you might bring some supporting material.

Bringing supporting materials to a meeting can also enhance the listener's perception of you as an expert in your subject matter. Remember, the person you're pitching to wants to know that you have passion for, and expertise in, your topic. If they ask you questions, you're expected to know the answers. Movie and television stories often take the viewer into unfamiliar worlds that are not part of our everyday lives. For example, if you were pitching our Spring Break EMT story, bringing props related to an EMT's specialized kit might help demonstrate that you have an expert understanding of their medical technology – but only if you then use the props to illustrate important story points. Otherwise they are likely to appear gimmicky or superfluous.

If you do decide to bring something, it should look professional. Remember, the people you're pitching to create media for a living. They're used to looking at the most high-quality materials. Unless you're a trained designer or artist, don't bring in drawings you made yourself. Most importantly, if you shoot a video, it must look professionally produced.

As we said earlier, it's common for reality and other non-fiction pitches to incorporate a sizzle reel. But again, it must be very well produced and edited, short, and compelling. It's also typical that a reality pitch might bring actual people as "props." If you're pitching another reality series with Kim Kardashian, by all means invite Kim to the meeting.

Directors are more likely than writers to bring visual aids to a pitch meeting. There are two things that directors will commonly use to support their pitches: a sizzle reel or a pitch book. Unlike a reality sizzle reel, a director's sizzle reel is cut together to show the visual style of the proposed project. Sometimes this is made up of original material, but more commonly it is footage assembled from other movies. Sometimes this kind of director's sizzle reel (sometimes called a "rip reel") will resemble a trailer. Rip reels are becoming more common as a prop for directors. A pitch book is a book of imagery – again, sometimes original, sometimes found. Like a sizzle reel, the purpose is to show the director's visual approach to the material. It is not necessary to produce either a director's sizzle reel or a pitch book, but if you do create something like this, the standard of professional quality still applies. It must look fantastic.

Sizzle Reels.

If you decide your pitch requires a sizzle reel there are a few things to think about before you create one. Of course, this presupposes that you, or someone you know, has the editing skills to create something that looks professional. If not, think twice before producing a reel.

As we've said, there are all kinds of sizzle reels – from non-narrative collages set to music to fully-narrative reels intended to sell a reality series, or perhaps a yet-to-be-made movie project on a crowdfunding website. Here are a few tips for organizing your reel:

- Understand what you are selling and know what the buyer/listener expects and/or needs to know about your project.
- Do your research. There are many other examples of sizzle reels available online. Some are very well made.
- Find a basic conceptual approach to your reel. How will your reel's content be organized? Is it narrative or non-narrative (a collage cut to music)? Is it a teaser? Is it a test reel or "mood" reel?
- What assets will you need? Are you creating/using original elements? Or are you creating your project out of pre-existing materials?
- Create a "script" for the work you hope to create, even if it's just a shot list. Sometimes you will want to create a script, then find or create the elements you will need to create the video. Other times you will have your elements beforehand and shape a script around them.

- Will your final product be self-explanatory or will you also need narration/voiceover or titles/cards? These elements must also be professional quality.
- Edit these things together in a *compelling* way. Remember why it's called a "sizzle reel": You're selling the sizzle, not the steak. Make it exciting, but not hyperbolic.
- Shorter is almost always better. In general, the less narrative, the shorter your reel should be. Most reels should run no more than two to five minutes. If there's no narrative (as with a cinematographer's reel), then two minutes is *plenty* long.
- Get input from trusted friends.
- Make changes based on their notes.
- Output final product in a variety of formats for your presentation: DVD, pen drive, and online, such as Vimeo. Remember, sometimes the playback device will not be yours. For example, you might be using your potential buyer's old DVD player. Plan for the possibility it might not work. Have a backup plan to present, even if it's just your iPad. Also, it's a good idea to always have a back-up copy in case your original media format fails. It happens.

"SPARTACUS"
by Grady Hall

I originally started out in the world of episodic writing, but had been exclusively directing music videos and commercials for about eight years when I heard that executive producers Sam Raimi, Rob Tapert, and Josh Donen were looking for someone to guide the launch, directing, and visual development of their new show for Starz – an R-rated, stylized, drama series fictionalizing the life of Spartacus.

At this early stage, there was no script or treatment – or at least not one anyone wanted to share. The most tangible concept about the series was that they wanted to do "television's first graphic novel series," and that the network loved the catchy idea that we were going to show gladiators as if they were "the NBA superstars of their time."

I had no credits they should care about, no recent series experience, and no previous connection to anyone involved. What I did have was a particular insight into visual storytelling, and about a month to prepare the answer to their dilemma: how exactly to create a high-quality "300"-style "graphic novel" look for around $2 million per episode. They agreed to meet with me.

In preparing for the pitch, instead of approaching it by thinking, "let me see if I can get this job," my thought was "when I start the job, I want to be ready to do it right." I acted as if I was already on the show – seeing every related film, watching behind-the-scenes visual effects clips, reading hundreds of graphic novels, devouring every historical, quasi-historical, and fictional work related to Spartacus and ancient Rome, and finally, boiling it all down to a clear vision for a shooting style and approach that served the stories we wanted to tell.

Thanks to my "nuclear" over-preparation, a pitch meeting that started ice-cold thawed almost instantly, as I walked the executive producers through my vision and approach to the show. It was the biggest mood change I've ever seen from the start of a meeting to the finish, and I think it's because I wasn't just pitching to join their show, I was solving their most daunting creative and production challenges as if I were already a member of the team.

The actual pitch had a high-energy montage of great movie scenes and some cool concept art, but the difference-maker was a clear vision of the road forward, supported by more than a hundred specific, original, doable ideas for scenes. I gave out printed presentations with custom-made concept art, passed around a dozen heavily bookmarked graphic novels, and shared inspired scenes from other films. I spoke without notes for about 45 minutes, but was vigilant about seeking questions, gauging reactions, and adjusting my emphasis accordingly. I delivered enough visual style ideas to last for the life of the series but, more importantly, I energetically presented my core idea that any visual technique or style we use must serve storytelling, emotion, and character. I was asked for a visual approach, and I delivered a story-driven visual approach, which is exactly what they wanted. I did the work before I was on the show as if I was already working on the show, and that's how I got on the show.

The deal was done within days, and I was off to the first season as a Director and Producer on a show that would go on to several successful seasons. We ended up using lots of specific ideas from that first pitch, but the meeting's most vital contribution was the introduction of the mantra to always prioritize storytelling over style, even when working on a show whose initial goal was merely to bring a big-screen visual experience to pay cable.

Leave-Behinds.

Far more common than props for writers is the "leave-behind." As the name suggests, this is a printed summary of your pitch that you leave with the executive, buyer, or producer after you've pitched to them. As we mentioned previously, if you come to pitch with a detailed outline, there's a chance the listener will ask if you can leave it behind for them to read. The reason is that the listener may have to pitch the idea to other people at their company before deciding whether to move forward. Giving them a leave-behind helps them do this better.

On the other hand, it also gives those mysterious "other people" something to reject. Many writers refuse to do leave-behinds because they would rather have the opportunity to re-pitch the project for the other execs. Of course, there's no guarantee that will have that opportunity, but it's more likely to happen if you haven't already given a convenient summary for them to read. Or that's the theory, anyway.

If you do decide to give them a leave-behind, we strongly suggest that you do *not* give them your pitch notes, as these are usually just an outline for your use in the room. You should definitely not hand over your bullet point notes. Instead, we advise you to craft a special document, for just this purpose, and limit it to one page. That's all you really need and you don't want to get into a situation where you're writing for free. Remember that this is a sales document. It's more akin to the pitch itself than a treatment. It has to be exciting. It has to grab the reader the same way your pitch ought to grab the listener.

If you agree to a leave-behind, we suggest you actually not leave it behind at that moment. Send it a day or so later, after you've had time to think about it. This will allow you to tweak the story based on valuable feedback or insight you may have received in the room. If you're working with a producer, consult with them about strategy before sending anything to the buyer.

Sometimes people do outrageous things to make an impression – let's call them "stunts." And every once in a while, it works… but usually it doesn't.

Famously, when Microsoft developed a film script based on their popular videogame "Halo," they had an actor dressed as the Halo character Master Chief deliver the script to the Hollywood studios and then had the actor wait around while the script was read by the studio. The actor was a stunt, and for two hours the studios had a guy in a costume sitting in their waiting room, presumably reading the trades. It was a little weird and the script never sold.

Our advice is to just be professional. Ultimately, you will succeed or fail based on your ability to tell a compelling story. Focus on crafting and rehearsing the verbal part of your pitch rather than devising intricate gimmicks.

CONCLUSION

> In the beginning there was nothing. God said, 'Let there be light!' And there was light. There was still nothing, but you could see it a whole lot better.
> —Ellen DeGeneres

Ironically, the end of this book is really just the beginning. If you've followed our advice, and if you made the effort, and if you sold a pitch – wow, that's great! You created *something* from *nothing* and sold it to Hollywood. Now the hard work really begins. Now you have to write the thing, or direct the thing, or get it produced.

That's the job. Pitching was just the way you *got* the job, and this is part of the broader perspective we mentioned in our introduction. As we also said in our introduction, this is a book about pitching, not screenwriting. Screenwriting is a complex profession that involves a combination of technical know-how, language skills, narrative instincts and a grasp of the human condition in all its folly and splendor. It's not easy. In fact, it's really hard.

But if you took this book to heart, it's also possible the job just got a little easier. Think about pitching and think about the regiment this book required of you. The suggestions in this book encouraged you to analyze many of your narrative choices via the pitching process, with a clear eye and with a practical, market-oriented goal in mind. This is the DNA of your idea. It also encouraged you to factor in other non-narrative elements such as casting and other production related considerations.

While it might be a stretch to say this book will make you a better writer, or director, or producer, it's very possible it will make you a better *storyteller* and lead you to craft more marketable ideas and materials. After all, aspects of pitching, such as viable concept and castability, are not only desirable qualities for a pitch but also tend to be the qualities Hollywood looks for when they decide which scripts they want to produce. This is really what it's all about. And this truly is the broader perspective.

INDUSTRY SLANG

Agent: A person or organization legally empowered to represents someone with the purposed of procuring employment. Typically, agents are licensed and regulated by state government. They are sometimes referred to as "talent agents," although in the entertainment industry this phrase is more often used to refer to agents that represent actors. Reputable agents are also franchised by the respective Guilds.

An Assignment: A writing or directing job that involves working on someone else's project, such as a rewrite of someone else's script or adaptation of a book owned by someone else. All director jobs are assignments, unless the director originated the project and is attached to direct.

Attorney: Attorneys are regulated by state government and licensed by the Bar Association to practice law in the state where they work. Entertainment attorneys in Hollywood are specialists in many kinds of contract law related to artist and labor agreements, intellectual property, real estate law (locations) and other media related legal matters.

Baby Writer: A new writer, usually in television.

Boutique Agency: A smaller agency often specializing in only a few types of representation. For example, a boutique agency might only represent a select list of screenwriters, or they might only represent child actors.

Coverage: A written summary and evaluation of a script, teleplay or book. Active production companies commission experienced readers to read the material and write coverage to help the production company evaluate the film and television potential of the large volume of materials they are submitted for production consideration. Coverage usually includes a log line, story summary, and evaluation.

Development: A term in Hollywood that refers to the acquisition and improvement of stories, ideas, and scripts.

Development Deal: A legal agreement to develop projects for a production company, studio or similar entity.

Development Executive: An employee of a production company whose job responsibilities can include meeting writers, writing notes and coverage, and managing the workflow of scripts. Sometimes, female development executives are referred to pejoratively as "D-girls." Never use this phrase.

Development Hell: When the script development process goes wrong and/or becomes painfully protracted. Frequently, this is when the "improvement" results in the end product being unrecognizable when compared to how it started out.

Elevator Pitch: A slightly tongue-in-cheek term for a very short pitch. This is the version of a pitch you will want handy if, by some luck, you find yourself on a brief elevator ride with Steven Spielberg or some other important person in the entertainment industry. Notwithstanding the negative connotations of having a "captive audience," most creative professionals should have a well-rehearsed log line for their projects ready at all times, whether they ride elevators or not.

Execution Dependent: An idea that depends on quality execution to be successful. They are hard to sell as a pitch, and often must be spec'd. Most non-high-concept ideas are execution dependent.

Four-Quadrant: A Hollywood phrase used in marketing and distribution that refers to a film that will appeal to the widest possible audience. Collectively, the four quadrants are Young Men, Young Women, Older Men and Older Women.

Franchise: In television, it refers to the creative aspect of a series that allows the series to present related storylines every week and also be ongoing, season after season. In motion pictures, franchise typically means a film that can spawn sequels and valuable ancillary "spin-offs," such as merchandising and even theme park attractions. But these two definitions can overlap. For example, the television series "Star Trek" is one of the most successful franchises in history, having spawned numerous additional series but also many motion pictures.

General Meetings: Also known as "Generals" among writers and directors. A meeting with a studio, producer, or production company not related to a specific project, but rather just to get acquainted. Be prepared to pitch anyway.

High-Concept: A story idea that's appeal is easily summarized in a compelling sentence or two. Occasionally confused with "one liner" or "log line," although it is not the same thing. Some log lines are high concept; some are not.

Intellectual Property (aka I.P.): The generic term for creations of the mind that can be legally owned, including such things as books, screenplays, and characters. Most often, the term intellectual property is used pertaining to copyright, trademark and patent law.

Life Rights: A somewhat misleading phrase related to the collection of real and *inferred* rights held by living people. Life rights are commonly considered to include rights related to privacy, defamation, and publicity.

Log Line: Any short description of a movie or television project. In addition to being a core element of most pitches, a log line is typically also used for the listing or cataloging of the project in places like an online tracking board, a film festival directory, or in a publication like "TV Guide."

Manager: A person or organization whose primary function is to offer career guidance to their clients. Managers are unregulated by the state and are typically not permitted to solicit employment for their clients, although in practice they frequently do so. Unlike agents, managers are permitted to work as producer on their client's projects.

MPAA Rating: The Motion Picture Association of America is a Hollywood trade organization that, in addition to representing the business interests of the Hollywood studios, also offers a film rating service. The "G," "PG," "PG-13" and "R" ratings are the most familiar. The rating system for television was co-created by the MPAA, and its use by broadcasters and cable companies is voluntary.

Open Assignment: An assignment for which the studio or other production company is actively looking for a writer or director. When there's an open assignment, it's not unusual for many writers or directors to meet and present their "take."

Option: More accurately referred to as an "option/purchase agreement." An option/purchase agreement is legal agreement between two parties that grants one of the parties the exclusive right to purchase something – most often a book or screenplay – within a certain time period. The option price is usually significantly less expensive than the purchase price. The word option can also be used as a verb as in, "I optioned the screenplay for a year, hoping I can find someone to finance the film."

An Original: Another term for a spec script or other project that originated with the writer. The Academy of Motion Picture Arts and Sciences defines it as a script not based on previously published materials. The Writers Guild of America definition is similar, but allows originals to be based on "research," published or not.

OTT: An abbreviation for "Over the Top." Refers to standalone video providers that deliver content via the Internet (as opposed to the more traditional cable or broadcast delivery). Examples include HBO Go, Netflix, and CBS All Access.

Packaging: The process by which other creative personnel ("elements") are attached to scripts to enhance the script's marketability. Typical creative personnel include actors, directors and sometimes producers. Agents and producers typically arrange most packaging.

Pilot: A stand-alone first episode of a potential series that is used to sell the rest of the series. If a television show is given a direct-to-series order (as is done with most streaming and cable series), the initial episode is just referred to as "the first episode."

Pitch Book: (Sometimes called a "pitch deck.") A book or digital file with photos and art – often culled from outside sources, but sometimes original – that is used to convey various visual aspects of a movie, commercial, or other production during a pitch. Common for director pitches, rare for writer pitches.

Producer's Polish: Polite term for a free script revision performed by the writer that is based on producers' notes and done prior to submitting a draft of the script to the studio, network or production company that commissioned the work. This is frowned upon by the WGA because their official position is that writers must always be paid when they write for hire. That said, most writers will agree to do a producer's polish, and it can serve the same valuable purpose as a "trusted friend," improving the script. Sometimes called a "courtesy draft."

Sample Script: Also known as "a writing sample," a script that is used, not to sell, but rather as an example of the writer's work. Typically, sample scripts will be sent to buyers before a pitch meeting or a general meeting is scheduled.

Set Piece: In film, a big, spectacular or elaborately conceived scene, usually in a comedy or action film.

Show-Runner: The head writer on a television series, whose job typically also includes casting, hiring staff writers, directors and crew, and overseeing production and editing. The term was devised to distinguish between writers that might have the same credit on the series, usually Executive Producers.

Sizzle Reel: A short, lively video presentation, typically no more than three minutes, of footage that is sometimes original and sometimes culled from multiple existing sources. In some cases, it is intended to give a sense of the tone, mood and style of a project or – in the case of reality programming – character and story. Common for director pitches, rare for writer pitches. The term can also refer to a short collage of a director's (or some other visual artist's) work.

Spec: As a noun, it means a screenplay or teleplay written without guaranteed payment on the "speculation" that it will sell upon its completion. Can also be used as a verb, as in, "Are you going to spec that idea, or pitch it?"

Submission Release Agreement: A legal agreement that agencies, studios and other companies often require unrepresented writers to sign before the company will read the writer's script. If signed, the writer waives his or her right to sue in the event that the material is in any way similar to other material that the company has seen or produced or that the agency's clients have written or produced.

Tagline: A short and clever slogan or "catchphrase" used in advertising or associated with a product or brand.

Take: A "take" is unique perspective on an idea as presented by a writer or director. Example: "That writer pitched a great take on the book adaptation." This is crucially important to get an assignment.

Tracking Boards: Private online forums or discussion groups frequented by development executives and/or their assistants that track all scripts and pitches coming onto the marketplace (usually listed by log line).

The Trades: Film industry news sources. Deadline, The Hollywood Reporter, and Variety are the most well-known.

Trailer Moment: A really "cool" moment or line of dialog in a pitch or script that you can easily imagine in the movie's trailer. Trailer moments often try to capture "heroic," funny or compelling moments in a story. You want to include at least a couple of these in your pitches.

Territories: Agent-speak for studios or buyers. Example: "We'll pick one producer to take the spec into each territory." In foreign sales, it refers to certain countries or geographic regions.

Underlying Material: A phrase that refers to the intellectual property that is used as the basis for some other work. This may be a book, another screenplay, a comic book, another film (for a remake or sequel), or even a board game (as in "Battleship").

Wheelhouse: A term used in Hollywood to indicate someone's artistic "comfort zone." For example, if a writer has only written comedies and wants to pitch a drama, it would be said that drama is outside the writer's wheelhouse, making it tougher to sell.

Genres

Genre is a basic way to categorize types of movies and television in Hollywood. It's likely you describe movies in this way as well. Of course, most people know comedy and drama. But Hollywood uses a much broader vocabulary for identifying genre. To help you sound like a pro, here is a list of typical genres, sub-genres, and common genre combinations that we use in Hollywood.

Action ("Jack Reacher," "Baby Driver")
    Action Comedy ("Spy," "Central Intelligence")
    Post-apocalyptic Action ("Mad Max: Fury Road")
    Action-Adventure ("The Fast and the Furious")

Adventure ("Tomb Raider")
    Comedic Adventure ("Jumanji: Welcome to the Jungle")
    Fantasy Adventure ("Harry Potter," "Pirates of the Caribbean")

Romance
    Romantic Comedy ("The Big Sick")
    Romantic Drama ("Call Me by Your Name")
    Romantic Fantasy ("Beauty and the Beast")
    Erotic Romance ("Fifty Shades of Grey")

Science Fiction
    Sci-Fi Adventure ("Star Wars: The Last Jedi")
    Dystopian Sci-Fi ("Divergent," "Blade Runner 2049")
    Near-future Sci-Fi ("Ex Machina")
    Sci-Fi Thriller ("10 Cloverfield Lane")
    Sci-Fi Drama ("Arrival")

Drama ("Three Billboards Outside Ebbing, Missouri")
    Historical Drama ("Hidden Figures")
    Survival Drama ("The Mountain Between Us")
    Teen Drama ("The Fault in Our Stars")
    Coming of Age Drama ("Lady Bird")
    Biographical Drama/Biopic ("The Imitation Game;" "I, Tonya")

Thriller ("The Accountant")
    Erotic Thriller ("Basic Instinct")
    Medical Thriller ("Flatliners," "Contagion")
    Noir Thriller ("Pulp Fiction," "The Salton Sea")
    Police Thriller ("Se7en," "L.A. Confidential")

Spy Movie ("Kingsman")

Murder Mystery ("Murder on the Orient Express")

Horror ("Split," "It")
    Supernatural Horror ("Paranormal Activity," "The Conjuring")
    Horror Comedy ("Happy Death Day," "Sean of the Dead")
    Sci-Fi Horror ("Life," "Alien")

Musical ('Les Miserables")
    Musical Comedy ("Pitch Perfect')

Superhero ("Wonder Woman")
    Superhero Comedy ("Deadpool," "Hancock")

Family Film
    Family Drama ('Wonder," "A Dog's Purpose")
    Family Comedy ("Paddington")
    Animated Family Comedy ("Despicable Me," "The Boss Baby")

War Movie ("Dunkirk," "Saving Private Ryan")

Comedy
    Raunchy Comedy ("Bridesmaid," "Girls Trip")
    Satire ("Spinal Tap," "The Dictator")

Faith-Based Drama ("The Shack," "Miracles from Heaven")

Western ("The Magnificent Seven," "Hostiles")

There are some things to be aware of in the above list:
- The grouping of genres can be haphazard – for example we include Romantic Comedy under Romance, but it also would fall under Comedy.
- You can probably see that some genres are more popular than others, both in the number of movies made and in the size of the potential box office.
- Some films might be categorized in different ways. For example, "Kingsman" could be called a spy movie, a thriller, or an action movie. Given that some genres are

more popular than others, it is in your best interest to describe your story in the most commercial way (while still being accurate.)
- Some movies combine these genres in uncommon ways that we didn't include on our list. For example, "Passengers" would best be described as a "Sci-Fi Romance," but not too many other movies would fall into that category.

Genres in Television
    Family comedy ("Modern Family")
    Workplace comedy ("The Office")
    Police procedural ("NCIS")
    Docu-soap ("Keeping up with the Kardashians," "The Real Housewives of Beverly Hills")
    Bio-drama ("The Wizard of Lies")
    Political drama ("House of Cards")
    Medical drama ("Chicago Medical," "Gray's Anatomy")
    Teen Drama ("Pretty Little Liars")
    Soap ("General Hospital," "Gossip Girl")
    Anthology series ("Black Mirror")
    Legal Drama ("Bull," "Damages")
    Prestige Drama ("The Handmaids Tale")
    Science Fiction ("The Expanse," "Star Trek")
    Fantasy ("Once Upon a Time," "The Magicians")
    Horror ("Bates Motel," "The Walking Dead")
    Superhero ("Arrow," "Jessica Jones")

The television industry also sometimes uses the term "genre show" to refer to the combined genres of science fiction, fantasy, and horror. Writers of such shows are often called "genre writers."

Praise for "The Hollywood Pitching Bible"

"A lot of us muddle through, hoping like hell we know what we're doing when faced with selling our wares to the Powers That Be. With this book, the power is now in your hands. No more hoping and floundering the dark with your story. Hit the lights. Stop hoping. Know."
-David Simkins (Writer of "Adventures in Babysitting," "Grimm," "Warehouse 13")

"Luck, they say, is when preparation meets opportunity. Consider yourself lucky that Douglas Eboch & Ken Aguado have written a book that tells you not only how to achieve a screenwriting career, but also sustain it over time."
-Lem Dobbs (Screenwriter of "Dark City," "The Limey," "The Score," "Haywire")

"There's nothing else like this book out there – a practical, down to earth, common sense guide to the art and science of the pitch written by two guys who have years of experience in the trenches. It's not only full of spot on advice and technique, it also covers what to expect in the room, pitching etiquette, pitching movies vs. television – all in all it will make you a better storyteller."
-John Gray (Writer/Director of "The Ghost Whisperer")

"Nine companies passed on the "Liar Liar" pitch before we sold it four years later. If I'd read this book back then, we might have sold it four years earlier."
-Paul Guay (Writer, "Liar Liar," "Heartbreakers," "The Little Rascals")

"An essential book about an essential skill."
-Ross LaManna (Writer of "Rush Hour")

"Most writers find the pitching process to be quite nerve-wracking, and this long-overdue book will offer them great comfort and encouragement. Douglas Eboch and Ken Aguado break down every aspect of a pitch, from the development of an idea to the challenge of confidently facing a room full of stone-faced executives. Moreover, they stress the importance of making a real personal connection to your material. If you have an urgent need to tell a particular story, there isn't a buyer in the world who won't want to hear it."
-Ken Kwapis (Director of "He's Just Not That Into You," "Big Miracle")

"Ken Aguado and Doug Eboch are guys who walk the walk, and here they talk the talk. They know as well as anyone how to navigate the trickiest waters on the continent: Hollywood's pitching process. Demystifying the secrets of what works and what doesn't for the not-so-brave new world of corporate Movie Biz. It's on my top shelf of books I can't be without."
-John Badham (Director of "Saturday Night Fever," "WarGames," "Stakeout")

"Salesmanship is not writing but it can be necessary/important so best do it well. 'The Hollywood Pitching Bible' is a superb guide to an unfortunate duty."
-David Peoples & Janet Peoples (Writers together and separately of such films as "12 Monkeys," "The Day After Trinity," "Unforgiven" and "Hero")

Made in the USA
San Bernardino, CA
13 April 2019